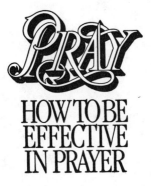

HOW TO BE
EFFECTIVE
IN PRAYER

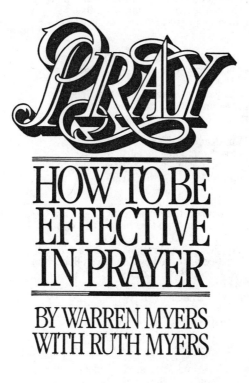

HOW TO BE EFFECTIVE IN PRAYER

BY WARREN MYERS
WITH RUTH MYERS

NAVPRESS

A MINISTRY OF THE NAVIGATORS
P.O. Box 6000, Colorado Springs, CO 80934

The Navigators is an international, evangelical Christian organization. Jesus Christ gave his followers the Great Commission to go and make disciples (Matthew 28:19). The aim of The Navigators is to help fulfill that commission by multiplying laborers for Christ in every nation.

NavPress is the publishing ministry of The Navigators. NavPress publications are tools to help Christians grow. Although publications alone cannot make disciples or change lives, they can help believers learn biblical discipleship, and apply what they learn to their lives and ministries.

Unless otherwise noted, all Scripture quotations are from the *New American Standard Bible,* © 1960, 1962, 1963, 1968, 1971, 1972, 1973, and 1975 by The Lockman Foundation. Other versions quoted are *The Amplified Bible* (AMP), © 1965 by Zondervan Publishing House; the *Good News Bible: Today's English Version* (TEV), © 1976 by the American Bible Society; the *King James Version* (KJV); *The Living Bible* (LB), © 1971 by Tyndale House Publishers; the *Holy Bible: New International Version* (NIV), © 1978 by the New York International Bible Society, and used by permission of Zondervan Bible Publishers; *The New Testament in Modern English, Revised Edition* (PH), © 1958, 1960, 1972 by J. B. Phillips; and *The New Testament: In the Language of the People* (Williams), © 1949 by Moody Bible Institute of Chicago.

Printed in the United States of America

Contents

Foreword   xiii

Introduction: Two Remarkable People   xv

Part I: Principles of Prayer   **1**

     1   God Honors Prayer   3

     2   Abiding—The First Foundation of Prayer   9

     3   Cleansing—The Second Foundation of Prayer   15

     4   The Three Conditions of Prayer   25

Part II: A Pattern of Prayer   **37**

     5   Thy Name, Thy Kingdom, Thy Will   39

     6   Our Daily Bread   47

     7   Forgive Us Our Sins   51

     8   Deliver Us   55

     9   The Kingdom, the Power, and the Glory   59

Part III: The Practice of Prayer   **63**

    10   Keeping a Quiet Time   65

    11   Improving Your Quiet Time   73

    12   Mining Riches from God's Word   79

    13   Our Emotions and God's Word   85

    14   Devotion and Commitment   97

    15   Make Time for Prayer   103

    16   Pray Anytime, Anywhere   111

    17   Keep On Asking   119

    18   Depend on the Holy Spirit   127

    19   Pray for the Lost   133

    20   Develop a Global Vision   139

Appendix A: Planning Your Quiet Time   145

Appendix B: Remarkable Answers and Persistence   149

Further Reading on Prayer   153

Index of Topics   155

Index of Scripture References   165

Index of Quotations and References to People   169

*To Dr. Robert Boyd Munger—
counselor, pastor, and friend—
whose prayers and example
laid deep foundations in my life.*

Author

Warren Myers received Jesus Christ as his personal Savior shortly before the end of World War II, while serving in the U.S. Army Air Corps. Following the war, he attended the University of California at Berkeley. He graduated in 1949 after studying religion and mechanical engineering, and was trained by The Navigators for three years as he served on the staff of the First Presbyterian Church of Berkeley.

In 1952 he went to Asia for The Navigators, serving in Hong Kong, India, and Vietnam before returning to a position in the United States in 1960. He has represented The Navigators in Singapore since 1970.

Warren and his wife, Ruth, have written three Bible studies on the person of God: *Experiencing God's Attributes, Experiencing God's Presence,* and *Discovering God's Will.*

Acknowledgments

The help and wise counsel of many have contributed to this book. My brother-in-law Jake Barnett, along with Paul Hensley, John Ridgway, and Mary Dawson, invested hours helping clarify and refine the manuscript. My son, Brian, did the painstaking work of producing the index. Ruth Hartman Ridgway wholeheartedly gave herself to typing and retyping the drafts. For their involvement and the help of others I am deeply grateful.

Foreword

It is with great pleasure that I pen the foreword to this book, written by my friend Warren Myers in a missionary situation in which prayer is an all-important component.

Prayer is both an ordinance and an art, and an art involves participation, not only native gift. It is more than a theory and can be mastered only by persevering practice. While this book treats the theory of prayer with keen insight, permeating the whole is the impression that the author has proved the theory in his own life. This adds to the book's authority.

Since this is the first volume in a trilogy, its scope is limited, and we can look forward with anticipation to the other volumes, which will fill out the picture. There is throughout the pages of this book the evidence of careful thought and research. When the trilogy is complete, it may well become a modern classic on prayer.

Although its aim is essentially practical, the volume rightly presents first the essential principles on which the possibility of prayer is based. This is followed by a helpful exposition of the Lord's Prayer, in which those principles are enshrined. The final section leads on to the practice of prayer—practical steps that, if taken, will lead to a well-rounded prayer life.

I foresee for this and the two succeeding volumes a most valuable and far-spreading ministry.

J. Oswald Sanders

Two Remarkable People

Nearly two centuries ago a shoe repairman in England became concerned about the non-Christian people of the world. Day after day, as he pounded on shoes, he prayed over a world map hung above his workbench. On the map he pasted facts gleaned from *Captain Cook's Travels*[1] and other secular books.

The time came when the praying cobbler felt he should act. As a lay preacher, William Carey urged his fellow Baptist ministers to become concerned about the world's unreached peoples. In 1792 he preached a sermon challenging them on their worldwide responsibility, and received the response, "Young man, sit down! When God wants to save the heathen, He will do it without your help or mine!"

Carey then told his wife that God was leading him to India. She refused to go with him or to let the children go. The East India Company denied him passage, warning him that if he managed to board one of their ships, they would not let him off in India. As he persisted with his vision, regarded by many as a wild dream, his father declared him mentally unbalanced.

In spite of such obstacles, and accompanied at the last moment by his wife and children, he obtained passage on a Danish ship. In 1793 they landed at the Danish colony of Serampore, near Calcutta, India, and William Carey was on his way to becoming the father of modern missions. This self-educated lay preacher who claimed, "I am not gifted, but I can plod," was used by God to change the course of world history.

Carey labored in India for forty-two years without a furlough. While working to support himself and others, and leading a wide and fruitful ministry, he and his co-workers translated the whole Bible into twenty-five Indian languages, the New Testament into eight more, and parts of the New Testament into seven others. They introduced God's Word into forty new languages—a task unequalled in missionary history.

When Carey landed in Serampore, only a few hundred missionaries were working in a few dozen countries of the world. Within twenty years of his arrival in India the Baptist Missionary Society, the London Missionary Society, the New York Missionary Society, the Church Missionary Society, The British and Foreign Bible Society, the American Board for Foreign Missions, and other missions sprang up and sent missionaries around the world. Today 68,000 Protestant missionaries labor in most of the world's countries, and the church of Jesus Christ has been planted in all but a few. The spark for this expanding outreach came through the writings, prayers, and example of an untrained plodder who lived by his motto, "Expect great things from God. Attempt great things for God."

Many books have been written about William Carey. No books have been written about his sister. Why would anyone write about her? She was "useless," almost totally paralyzed for fifty-two years. But she was close to God and close to her brother. He wrote her the details of his struggles in writing grammar books, primers, and dictionaries. He described the difficulties of founding type and printing Bibles. He also sent her letters telling about starting newspapers to promote literacy, establishing schools, training teachers, founding churches, and educating pastors to care for the converts God gave them. He sent the details to his bedridden sister in London, and hour after hour, month after month, she lifted those details to the Lord in prayer.

To whose account will God credit the victories won through this remarkable man? How will He divide the rewards? David stated in 1 Samuel, "As his share is who goes down to the battle, so shall his share be who stays by the baggage; they shall share alike."[2] Does not this principle of physical warfare for ancient Israel also apply to our spiritual warfare? A bedridden sister shares her famous brother's rewards. An engineering student, an executive, or a mother who prays has a world-changing influence, rich in rewards, without leaving home or country. J. O. Fraser wrote,

> Many of us cannot reach the mission fields on our feet, but we ✓ can reach them on our knees. Solid lasting missionary work is accomplished by prayer, whether offered in China, India, or the United States.

When God invites us to pray, He offers us an extraordinary opportunity. Prayer can change our circumstances and bring God's transforming power into our lives, but it does far more. Prayer gives us the opportunity to link our lives with God's broad purposes for the world. For why are we here? Is it not to have on our hearts what God has on His heart—our secular, sinful, needy world—and to have a part in reaching it?

The Purpose of this Book

My prayer is that this book will motivate you and deepen your understanding. But most of all I trust this book will help you to pray. It is a book that will reward prayerful reflection. If you choose to read through the book rapidly, return to it as a practical handbook, reading one chapter at a time and applying its truths before pressing on to the next. Allow a week for the chapters in parts I and II, and two weeks for most chapters in part III. This will help you establish in your life the scriptural principles and the practical suggestions in the chapters, many of which encourage you to pause and pray immediately, putting into practice what you have just read.

As the Lord enables you to apply His principles and the book's suggestions, you will pray more and more effectively, and you will join those who influence the world.

The great people of the earth today are the people who pray. I do not mean those who talk about prayer; nor those who say they believe in prayer; nor yet those who can explain about prayer; but I mean those people who _take_ time and _pray_. They have not time. It must be taken from something else. This something else is important. Very important, and pressing, but still less important and less pressing than prayer.[3]

NOTES   1. Captain James Cook, the courageous explorer, sailed around the world in the early 1770s and wrote a detailed account of many lands and peoples.
2. 1 Samuel 30:24.
3. S. D. Gordon, _Quiet Talks on Prayer_ (Grossett and Dunlap, 1904), page 12.

PART I
Principles of Prayer

God wants us to pray with confidence and effectiveness, and tells us how to do so. Part I develops the essentials of effective prayer, giving special attention to its twin foundations and its three conditions.

1

God Honors Prayer

Thou art coming to a King.
Large petitions with thee bring,
For His grace and power are such
None can ever ask too much.
—An old hymn

Who is this King to whom we come in prayer? He is the eternal God, creator and sustainer of everything, everywhere. He reigns over the celestial universe, guiding the stars and planets in their courses, calling each star by name. He also governs the microscopic universe, holding together every atom in every cell of our bodies. He numbers the hairs of our heads. He cares about us. Augustine, one of the early church fathers, declared, "He loves us every one as though there were but one of us to love."

To such a God we can never bring requests that are too large or too small.

God Answers Specific Prayer

Laurens Pantouw was preparing to leave Indonesia, his tropical homeland, to spend the winter in Japan. Having resigned from a good job to serve the Lord, he had little money and many needs. So he prayed to his rich and generous heavenly Father for the specific things he needed.

Just before Laurens left Bandung, a missionary friend inquired about his needs. Laurens told how he had prayed for white shirts to wear with the neckties required in Japan, for shoes to replace his tropical sandals, and for a warm overcoat—a rare item in Indonesia. God had supplied each of these. As they were saying goodbye, the missionary remembered he had an extra suitcase. "Could you use it?" he asked. "It's one we won't need."

Laurens smiled. "Yes, that was the last thing on my list, to carry the other things I asked the Lord for." Happily helpless and dependent, Laurens found God sufficient.

God honors prayer. He rewarded Laurens's prayer for specific needs, and He yearns to do the same for us. He longs to demonstrate His power in the tremendous trials that jar us like thunder, and in the pinprick troubles that annoy us. Giant needs are never too great for His power; dwarf-sized ones are never too small for His love. As the apostle Paul told the Philippians, "Be anxious for nothing, but in everything by prayer and supplication with thanksgiving let your requests be made known to God."[1]

God can answer prayer because He is the supreme ruler of all. Some earthly monarchs reign, but they do not govern. But God reigns *and* governs. He governs both world events and our individual lives, ready at our request to act, to intervene, to overrule for our good, His glory, and the progress of the gospel.[2] He has decreed that prayer is the way to secure His aid and move His mighty hand. Therefore even in sickness, failure, rejection, or financial distress, we can pray and experience His peace which transcends human understanding. Through prayer we can open a window to let God's love shine into our lives; we can open our hands to receive His riches; we can open our hearts to let His presence fill and empower us. Through it we can also allow Him to provide answers to prayer that are important to Him and to us.

S. D. Gordon tells of an interview he had with a Midwestern congressman who for years had lectured vehemently against the existence of God. The congressman related, "I was sitting at my desk in Congress listening to an exciting debate—not a time to think about one's soul—when there came to me a distinct impression that God was there looking at me, and that He was displeased with my attitude toward Himself."

He said to himself, "This is ridiculous. I am getting morbid.

I have been working too hard. I will have a long walk in the fresh air and a good meal, and get rid of this absurd impression."

But when he returned to his seat, the impression returned—"God, there, looking at me." Day after day for weeks the awareness continued.

He then had occasion to return to his home in the Midwest.

"The greetings were over with my wife," he said, "and I was quietly resting, when she said in a very tactful way, 'Henry, two of us have made a covenant of prayer that you shall become a Christian, and the real kind.'" Instantly he thought about that strange experience in Washington.

Pretending indifference, he asked her when "this praying thing" had begun. She named the date.

"I knew in a moment," he told Gordon, "that she had named the date when the impression came to me for the first time. I was tremendously shaken. I was honest; I believed there was no God. But I was a lawyer, and here was a bit of evidence. When those two women did something they called praying, on the banks of the Mississippi, something happened to me two thousand miles away."

The next night he went to church with his wife. At the close of the service, when the opportunity was given, he walked down the aisle. "Every step was breaking a precedent. Every step said, 'I have been wrong.'" But he walked down, knelt, "and made the simple surrender of his strong will to the Higher will."[3]

Scriptural praying covers both momentous matters and trifles. We are to pray for men and women to be converted to Christ and to mature. We are to pray about a lost key and pesky insects. God answers specific prayer. He saves the spiritually lost who call on Him in prayer. He provides shirts and suitcases and salvation for people in need.

Prayer Is Simple and Enjoyable
Prayer is more than making requests. It is talking with our Father, sharing our thoughts and feelings, our appreciation, our doubts, our problems, our complaints. It includes confessing sin, committing ourselves to obey God, worshipping, praising, and giving thanks for His blessings and provisions.

GOD HONORS PRAYER

If we can talk, we can pray. Prayer no more requires a special vocabulary or tone of voice than does talking to our friends. If we feel more comfortable with formal ways of speaking to God, such as "Thee" and "Thou," He is delighted to hear us. If we prefer the informal "You" and a reverent casualness, this too pleases Him, and is consistent with the casual, everyday Greek in which the New Testament was written. God loves to hear our voice. He is grieved by our silence.

Prayer usually involves words, whether thought or whispered, sung or shouted. Yet at times prayer is just a moment of quietness directed toward God. At other times it is repeated groanings, questions, or pleas as we pour out our heart before Him.[4] Often we can pray briefly as we are working or walking, merely saying, "Lord, I'm confused. Please help me," or "Thank you, Father. That worked out well." True prayer always involves a heart turned Godward.

Prayer can bring us much enjoyment as we experience specific answers to our requests. "Ask, and you will receive, that your joy may be made full."[5] However, the subjective benefits of prayer that happen in us as we pray offer even greater joy. Through prayer we know God better and our values change. He becomes our "exceeding joy,"[6] and doing His will becomes our chief delight.

Relating to Him in prayer changes our characters. Month after month, year after year, He transforms our thinking, our attitudes, our actions. These subjective benefits blend with the objective answers to increase our enjoyment of prayer. We may not sense these benefits as we first begin to pray, but they come as we develop our prayer life.

Prayer is simple, but maturity in prayer comes from time and practice. There are few shortcuts, so we need to be patient as we grow in our prayer life, not giving up if we do not experience immediate enjoyment and exciting answers. God does not expect instant maturity in prayer. A child does not start his education with postgraduate studies. Be patient with yourself and God.

Our understanding of prayer increases as we grow spiritually, yet no human being has totally resolved the mysteries of prayer. As in many of our activities, we can proceed successfully without full understanding. Most people learn to drive a car without grasping the intricacies of the engine; most use electricity without knowing the physical laws involved. Likewise we can learn to pray effectively though we cannot plumb all the mysteries of why and how prayer moves God's mighty hand.

Why not pause now and ask the Lord to teach you to pray with growing effectiveness, as S. D. Gordon did: "Lord Jesus, teach us to pray. . . . Thou knowest both ends of prayer, the praying end down here, and the answering end up yonder. Teach us."[7]

Confidence in Prayer
Prayer furnishes the incredible privilege of coming boldly to the great, living God to enjoy His presence and make our petitions. We can come with confidence to "receive mercy [for our failures] and . . . appropriate help and well-timed help, coming just when we need it."[8] Why do we have such freedom to approach the holy God, the King of the universe?

Our Lord Jesus Christ, through His death and resurrection, has cancelled all our sins—past, present, and future.[9] He knew the malignancy of sin in our lives and He was willing to suffer sin's penalty in our place. "He was pierced for our transgressions, He was crushed for our iniquities; the punishment that brought us peace was upon Him, and by His wounds we are healed."[10]

When godless men nailed Jesus to the cross and let Him die, evil appeared to have triumphed. But to the joy of His followers and the dismay of His enemies, death could not hold Him in its grasp. In a mighty demonstration of power, God raised Him from the dead, publicly declaring Him to be His Son. By that same power He enthroned Him in the position of supreme honor in heaven.

Through faith in Christ Jesus crucified and risen, we have become children of God, totally forgiven by Him who promises, "I, even I, am the one who wipes out your transgressions for My own sake; and I will not remember your sins."[11] Now we have perfect standing with God through Jesus Christ. As we come in His merits, it is as though Jesus Himself were making the requests. Through Him we are insiders in the court of heaven. "Now, through the blood of Christ, you who were once outside . . . are with us inside the circle of God's love in Christ Jesus. . . . It is in this same Jesus, because we have faith in Him, that we dare, even with confidence, to approach God.[12]

> Now you are no longer strangers to God and foreigners to heaven, but you are members of God's very own family, citizens of God's country, and you belong in God's household with every other Christian.[13]

Prayer sets our feet in our new homeland and lets us breathe its air. Our Father, who thinks of us constantly, eagerly awaits our every visit home, whether we come for a few minutes, a half hour, or an afternoon. Isn't it strange that we find it hard to tear ourselves away from the polluted air of the world to spend time in the invigorating atmosphere of our true homeland, that we live our lives near the spiritual poverty line, when God wants to lavish His gifts on us and meet our every need.

NOTES
1. Philippians 4:6.
2. Philippians 1:12.
3. S. D. Gordon, *Five Laws that Govern Prayer* (Fleming H. Revell, 1925), pages 16–19.
4. Psalm 62:8.
5. John 16:24.
6. Psalm 43:4.
7. S. D. Gordon, *Quiet Talks on How to Pray* (Fleming H. Revell, 1929), page 23.
8. Hebrews 4:16, AMP.
9. Hebrews 10:14.
10. Isaiah 53:5, NIV.
11. Isaiah 43:25.
12. Ephesians 2:13, PH.
13. Ephesians 2:19, *The Living Bible.*

Abiding—the First Foundation of Prayer

> I am the vine, you are the
> branches; he who abides in Me,
> and I in him, he bears much
> fruit; for apart from Me
> you can do nothing.
> (John 15:5)

Abiding in Christ and *being cleansed* of known sin form twin foundations for effective prayer. Abiding is the spring from which scriptural praying flows. Being cleansed prevents sin from damming up the spring.

Abide in Christ
Abiding in Christ is essential for prayer that pleases God and brings answers. Trying to cultivate prayer without abiding in Christ is like trying to grow palm trees in Siberia. The climate is wrong.

Abiding means keeping our shared life with Christ harmonious, free from the discord of sin. It is closely related to cherishing and obeying His Word: "If you abide in Me, and My words abide in you, ask whatever you wish, and it shall be done for you."[1]

A vine sustains its branches so that they bear grapes. So Christ, as we abide in Him, provides the life and strength we need for obedient, productive lives, as well as for effective prayer.

Abiding kindles within us a craving for the greatest gift we can receive through prayer, a richer experience of God Himself. Whatever else He gives is secondary. In the fourth century Augustine prayed, "Give me Your own self, without whom, though You should give me all that ever You have made, yet could not my desires be satisfied."

Abiding means we will experience intimate fellowship with the King. This is the crowning privilege of being a member of His kingdom and family.

Some years ago a gifted young Australian named John Ridgway was selected by his government to personally tutor the Crown Prince of Thailand, who was soon to attend Australia's Royal Military Academy. John lived with the King of Thailand and his family. He enjoyed the distinction of being an insider in a family with almost unlimited privilege and veneration among the Thais— a unique honor. He traveled with the royal family, lived in their palaces, and fellowshipped with them. He ate with them daily and enjoyed their special delicacies, the banquets, and state dinners. He viewed firsthand the crowns and jewels, the gold and riches of royalty. But this privilege was only temporary. He was a short-term guest, not a permanent family member.

When we welcomed Jesus Christ into our heart as Savior and Lord, He welcomed us into His Father's family as permanent members. We were born as royal children with full status and privileges, joint heirs with the Son of God Himself.[2]

The privileges of royalty, ours by birth, become ours in *practice* as we learn of them in God's Word and make them our own through faith and obedience. The more we share Christ's life and let Him share ours, the more we enjoy the full benefits of being branches in the vine, members of His body, sharers of His divine nature. We tap into His twenty-four-hour-a-day protection, strength, guidance, and comradeship.

How does abiding affect our praying? As we cultivate our intimacy with Christ, He remolds our thoughts and desires, aligning them with His own. Then both knowing and desiring what He wants, we ask for that alone, and He answers our prayers. "Delight yourself in the Lord; and He will give you the desires of your heart."[3] At times God even answers the prayers of people who do not know Him personally. But a *life* of answered prayer springs from happy dependence in which God and the person are intimately bound together in daily companionship.

Abiding Is Simple

Colossians 2:6 gives the secret of abiding, of living our lives in Christ: "So, just as you once accepted Christ Jesus as your Lord, you must continue living in vital union with Him."[4]

How did we receive Christ? Through humility and faith. We humbly admitted that we were sinners and that our works were inadequate to earn eternal life. Consciously or not, we laid aside our pride and humbled ourselves before Him as our Lord. We received Him by faith, trusting Him to save us, and He entered our hearts, bringing forgiveness and eternal life.

We abide in vital union with Him through the same kind of faith by which we received Him. In humility we agree with Jesus' words, "Apart from Me you can do nothing."[5] In our own strength we can achieve nothing of eternal significance. As a car cannot run without gas, or as a light bulb cannot shine without electricity, so we cannot serve or glorify God in our own strength. If we depend on our own insights and abilities, any "fruit" we produce is like artificial grapes tied to a vine. We cannot by ourselves produce genuine spiritual fruit.

Yet God does not intend us to face life with an "I–can't" attitude. Against the backdrop of our inadequacy, He wants us by faith to affirm our adequacy in Christ, to say as Paul did, "I can do all things through Him who strengthens me."[6]

Abiding in Christ is based on faith, on putting confidence in Him for strength and victory, for guidance and effectiveness. It is dependence rather than independence. It means relaxing and resting in Him amid the pressures and disturbances that plague our days. It means thinking and acting with the confidence that He is in control, not ourselves, or circumstances, or Satan. As we abide, we need not push and maneuver to work things out in frustrated self-effort. We need not retaliate when thwarted or inconvenienced or humiliated.

Abiding in Christ does not eliminate hard work or careful planning, nor does it exempt us from frustrating circumstances. Instead it enables us to go through our days and weeks with His peace reigning in our hearts. Abiding brings inward rest in spite of circumstances. It frees us from the turmoil of inner pressures and anxieties that come when we depend on anyone or anything other than Christ to accomplish both our tasks and His.

Abiding is based on a simple trust in Christ and a lack of trust in ourselves. Such faith and humility bring us an inner rest, described by Andrew Murray:

> Humility is perfect quietness of heart. It is never to be irritated or sore or disappointed. It is to expect nothing and to wonder at nothing that is done to me. It is to be at rest when nobody praises me and when I am blamed and despised. It is to have a blessed home in the Lord where I can be at rest when everything around and above is a sea of trouble.

We sustain our attitude of humility and faith through God's Word. As we continue to learn and agree with what He says, our abiding becomes more constant. Yet it is possible to feed on His Word and somehow still miss the simplicity of the resting life— unless by faith we depend on the truths He has revealed. Again and again, whenever we sense a need (as we begin a new day, start a new task, confess a failure) we must *choose* to trust Him as our life and sufficiency.

Hudson Taylor, though a dedicated missionary and head of the China Inland Mission, found himself going through darkness, failures, and futile struggles for holiness. He knew that all he needed was in Christ, but he wrestled with how to get it out of Christ into himself. Then one day it became clear. He realized that we abide in Christ not by determined self-effort but by restful faith, by fixing our eyes on Jesus.[7]

Taylor gathered his co-workers and told them, "I am one with Christ. It was all a mistake to try and get the fullness out of Him. I am part of Him. Each of us is a limb of His body, a branch of the vine."[8]

Later he wrote his sister, telling of the joy and peace that flowed as he realized the unchanging faithfulness of Jesus and His promise to be always with him and in him, ready to meet every need. He continued:

I saw not only that Jesus will never leave me, but that I am a member of His body, of His flesh and of His bones. The vine is not the root merely, but all—root, stem, branches, twigs, leaves, flowers, fruit. And Jesus is not that alone—He is soil and sunshine, air and showers, and ten thousand times more than we have ever dreamed, wished for, or needed. . . .

O, my dear Sister, it is a wonderful thing to be really one with a risen and exalted Saviour . . . I am no longer anxious about anything, as I realize this; for He, I know, is able to carry out His will, and His will is mine . . . No fear that His resources will prove unequal to any emergency! And His resources are mine, for He is mine, and is with me, and dwells in me.[9]

Years later, Mr. Taylor was asked if he was always conscious of abiding in Christ. He replied, "While sleeping last night, did I cease to abide in your home because I was unconscious of the fact? *We should never be conscious of not abiding in Christ.*"[10]

As we abide in Christ, He empowers us to do God's will and to bear fruit. The outworking of abiding includes persistent prayer, diligent study, and strenuous service. But these lose their strain as we cease from the burden of struggling in our own power to produce a restful, Christlike life that glorifies God.

If you have longed in vain for a full, abiding life, begin to pray regularly about your need. Ask the Lord to help you understand how to abide by simple faith. Ask Him to show you any sin that is blinding you or choking off the powerful life of the Vine.

Perhaps God is waiting to deliver you from some habitual sin such as self-pity or a resentful, unforgiving spirit. If we have entwined our personalities around such attitudes, we are often blind to their presence. Or the hindrance can be an independent spirit or self-sufficiency that has not submitted to the truth, "Apart from Me you can do nothing." Ask God to clarify your understanding, to search your heart, to remove any hindrance preventing His full control. "Every one who asks and keeps on asking receives, and he who seeks and keeps on seeking finds."[11]

Review the last paragraph, asking God to show you anything that needs confessing and cleansing. As God enables you to abide in Christ more fully, the apostle John's words will become true in your life: "Dear friends, if our hearts do not condemn us, we have confidence before God and receive from Him anything we ask, because we obey His commands and do what pleases Him."[12]

NOTES
1. John 15:7.
2. Romans 8:16–17.
3. Psalm 37:4.
4. Williams translation.
5. John 15:5.
6. Philippians 4:13.
7. Hebrews 12:2.
8. John Pollock, *Hudson Taylor and Maria* (Zondervan Publishing House, 1962), page 198.
9. Dr. and Mrs. Howard Taylor, *Hudson Taylor's Spiritual Secret* (London: China Inland Mission, 1935), pages 115–116.
10. Taylor, page 116.
11. Luke 11:10, AMP.
12. 1 John 3:21–22, NIV.

3

Cleansing—the Second Foundation of Prayer

*I acknowledged my sin to Thee,
and my iniquity I did not hide;
I said, "I will confess
my transgressions to the Lord";
and Thou didst forgive
the guilt of my sin.*
(Psalm 32:5)

Abiding in Christ depends on continual cleansing. Only Jesus lived a totally abiding life and never needed forgiveness. Each of us needs frequent forgiveness and renewal in order to maintain our closeness to Him.

If your child disobeys you by running outside on a rainy day, and comes back covered with mud, he does not lose his family membership. But you do not invite him to sit down, join the family, and have his dinner. Not yet. First he needs cleansing, not a re-adoption or rebirth, but simply a washing. Plenty of soap and water, clean clothes, and he is ready for dinnertime fellowship.

So it is with us. Sin breaks our fellowship with God. It does not destroy our permanent relationship, but it does rob us of our enjoyment of His presence until we are cleansed. "He who conceals his transgressions will not prosper, But he who confesses and forsakes them will find compassion."[1]

Sin Divides and Destroys

If not acknowledged and forsaken quickly, sin disrupts and damages relationships. Satan, the master strategist, uses sin as a wedge to pry apart families, study groups, ministry teams, committees, and even congregations. From a tiny beginning it can grow until it destroys not only our harmony with others, but also our intimacy with God and effectiveness in prayer.

For years a woman in our church walked with increasing difficulty. Then one day she came to Bible class all smiles.

"Warren, it's wonderful," she said. "I had an operation last week and I'm enjoying walking for the first time in ten years."

"Ten years?"

"Yes, my feet had been getting more and more painful until finally I could only hobble. I was afraid of hospitals and put off the operation as long as I could. I was foolish to have waited so long. It's so good to be free of those miserable corns."

Sometimes we allow a sin to continue in our life for years. The longer we ignore the pain and put off the needed surgery, the more it destroys our spiritual vitality and deforms our personality until eventually we are almost disabled.

A friend of mine was lured into twenty-seven years in a spiritual wilderness through self-pity and resentment that mushroomed into bitterness. His reasons for feeling resentful were convincing. But his unforgiving spirit withered his fellowship with God, destroyed his Christian effectiveness, ruined his marriage, and damaged his children. Even if he had valid grounds for his attitude, he wasted twenty-seven years of his life trying to convince himself that he was right—a poor exchange.

Now he has been released and restored, having destroyed the separating barrier by admitting his sin of hidden bitterness. He is again experiencing the warmth of God's friendship, is back with his wife, and is finding abundant opportunities to help others.

Sin unacknowledged and unconfessed hinders not only our spiritual progress but also our emotional well-being, and through that, our physical health. Leading health authorities agree that the deeper causes of many illnesses are our emotional reactions to life. Prolonged bitter hatred can damage the brain and cause heart disorders, high blood pressure, and acute indigestion—all severe enough to kill a person! To hate is to willfully sabotage the fine mechanism of the human body.

He who conceals his sins does not prosper."[2] Sin erects walls between us and God and between us and others. If we continue to ignore or hide our offenses, the walls can become almost insurmountable. Such barriers damage the builder as much as those on the other side. When we are willing to admit our sin and ask for forgiveness, the walls come down and we are on our way to healing and blessing.

Sin Hinders Prayer

Sin breaks our intimacy with God, who will not hear us if we knowingly hold on to that which displeases Him.[3] It drains away our desire to know God's will and to pray in accordance with it. It is an ever-present overcast that shuts out the bright presence of our prayer-answering God.

God's people in Isaiah's day wondered why, though they prayed earnestly, God took no notice.[4] The prophet Isaiah knew why. He pointed out their critical spirit, their oppression of other people, their contention and strife, and their failure to draw themselves out to meet the needs of the hungry and afflicted. He reminded them that God was not dull of hearing or powerless to answer, but that their sins were blocking their prayers.[5] The solution Isaiah prescribed was to turn from their sins: "Then you will call, and the Lord will answer; You will cry, and He will say, 'Here I am.' "[6]

The apostle Peter points out that an unscriptural husband-wife relationship also hinders prayer. He urges husbands to live with their wives in an understanding and considerate way, and to honor them, "that your prayers may not be hindered."[7] Husbands have the heavy responsibility of cherishing their wives with Christlike love. This promotes effective praying. Wives also are to follow God's pattern, adapting and submitting to their husbands in order not to forfeit family harmony and answered prayer.[8]

Receiving God's Cleansing

When a friend of mine conducts weddings, he likes to remind the couple that the seven hardest words in the English language are, *I was wrong. Will you forgive me?* Although this exhortation may not be necessary before the wedding, it seldom takes a couple long afterward to discover its importance.

When we need cleansing, the first step is to ask God for forgiveness. It is amazing how fast this lowers inner pressures and tensions. A young man in Burma who for months had been afraid he was losing his mind finally admitted his sin openly and prayed for forgiveness. A short time later he glowingly remarked, "God has given me back my mind." He was cleansed and inwardly released, having taken his first step toward emotional healing.

Psalm 32:5, quoted at the beginning of this chapter, illustrates the simplicity of confession. You need not go through a complicated ceremony, but merely stop hiding the sin and acknowledge it to the Lord. Do not defend yourself or offer excuses. Admit to God exactly what you have done, call it sin, and ask His forgiveness. "If we confess our sins, He is *faithful* and *just* and will forgive us our sins and purify us from all unrighteousness."[9]

God is faithful. He keeps His promises, and He longs to restore us to intimate friendship with Himself. When we acknowledge our sin and accept His cleansing, His total reliability guarantees us freedom from the contamination of sin in our personalities.

God is also justified in forgiving and forgetting our failures because the total debt for all our sin was paid on the cross. God actually made His sinless Son to be sin on our behalf, that we might be made righteous.[10]

When we received eternal life in Christ, and with it full forgiveness, the greatest trade in history took place. We traded our corruption for His perfection, our terminal illness for His unending life, our alienation for His warm welcome.

Now God will never again charge sin to our account. There is nothing more to do, no further payment to make. God would be unjust to demand a second payment, and we grieve Him if we try to make one in any way. We need only to ask God to forgive the specific sin that has broken our fellowship, and He cleanses and restores us. We do not deserve this. We need not earn it. It is ours because of His just provision and promise.

As Jesus washed His disciples' feet in John 13, He taught not only humble service, but also complete spiritual cleansing. When He dressed Himself as a servant and began this menial task, Peter objected. But Christ warned him, "If I do not wash you, you have no part with Me."[11] Then Peter wanted a complete bath.

At this point Christ revealed the spiritual lesson of the foot washing. "He who has bathed needs only to wash his feet, but *is completely clean;* and you are clean, but not all of you."[12]

One of his disciples was spiritually unclean. Though he joined the activities and fellowship of the disciples, Judas lacked the faith in Christ necessary for cleansing. The rest of the disciples had been spiritually cleansed and did not need a second or third or fourth spiritual bath or rebirth.

We, too, having been born again, are completely clean. We need only to wash the part that gets dirty in daily life. We need only to turn to the Lord as often as necessary and say, "I was wrong. Please forgive me."

There was a time in my life when I wondered if God would really forgive me just on the basis of my asking. It seemed too easy. Did I not need to demonstrate my sincerity, at least putting myself on temporary probation? This seemed more logical. How liberating it was to discard my "reasonable" idea, which conflicted with God's Word: "He who has bathed needs only to wash his feet."

The spiritual cleansing symbolized by footwashing takes only a brief prayer: "Father, forgive me for my complaining spirit." "Forgive me for my unclean thinking." "Forgive me for doubting You." Then, based on His promises, we are again clean and restored.

Is there some sin you need to confess in order to live without guilt and pray boldly? Ask the Lord to reveal it, then confess it immediately and be clean. Perhaps Suzannah Wesley's definition of sin will help you.

> Whatever weakens your reason, impairs the tenderness of your conscience, obscures your sense of God, or takes away the relish for spiritual things; in short, whatever increases the strength and authority of your body over your mind—that thing is sin to you[13]

Confession Requires Humility

Many sins are only against God and need confessing to Him alone. If the sin involves others, we must go to each person involved (but not beyond the circle that our sin has affected) and say, "I was wrong. Will you forgive me?"

As a missionary I find it humiliating to go to my wife or my children and ask them to forgive me for being angry, impatient, unkind, domineering, or critical of their motives. Though I have walked with the Lord for over thirty years, I still need frequent cleansing. My old nature no longer controls me in many of the ways it used to, but I still have painful-but-delightful opportunities to let God apply the spiritual soap of 1 John 1:9. Christian workers sometimes hesitate to admit sin, feeling this lowers them in the eyes of their followers or of others. Actually, quick confession wins their respect. When I confess anger or impatience to my wife, it is no surprise to her. The surprise may be that it took me so long to acknowledge it. Though confessing is difficult, it is worth the cost. It removes my feelings of guilt and restores my intimacy with God and my inner peace.

Due to an irritating airport delay a well-known Bible teacher became angry with an airline ticket agent. After stewing for some time in self-justification, he returned and asked the man to forgive him, commenting, "I am a Christian and shouldn't have acted like that." The ticket agent responded, "I am too. That's why I can take all the remarks that people make!"

The first move in reconciliation is always our responsibility, regardless of who has committed the offense. If we are guilty, we are responsible to go to the person offended and ask forgiveness. "If therefore you are presenting your offering at the altar, and there remember that your brother has something against you, leave your offering there before the altar, and go your way; first be reconciled to your brother, and then come and present your offering."[13]

If we have stolen, told a lie, or spoken critically of someone else, we must make restitution to that person as well as ask God's forgiveness. Restitution can take many forms: repaying money, admitting the truth, seeking to repair a reputation we have damaged. One teenager said to his sister, "I've been treating you as though you were a nobody, and this is sin because you are important and I appreciate you. Will you forgive me?" He not only asked forgiveness but also took a step toward restoring what he had been stealing from her—her self-esteem.

Both Peter and James point out that God resists the proud but gives grace to the humble.[14] Facing a sin *shows* humility and *develops* humility. It brings new grace and gives fresh confidence to pray boldly.

In seeking reconciliation, it helps to ask, "Will you forgive me?" This encourages the person to forgive and to acknowledge that he does so. And when someone asks us for forgiveness, we should *say* that we forgive them. Such two-way verbal settling of accounts helps to close an issue. My wife and I make a practice of saying, "Yes, I forgive you," rather than just, "Oh, it's all right." We avoid responses that minimize the sin or sidestep the hard choice to forgive.

When someone has done something against us, should he not come to us and ask forgiveness? Yes, but if he does not, the first move is our responsibility: "If a brother sins against you, go to him privately and confront him with his fault. If he listens and confesses it, you have won back a brother."[15]

When we are aware of a sin in a fellow believer, we should gently and humbly point it out and seek to restore the person. This is one way of washing another's feet and helping him bear his burden.[16]

Admit Sin Quickly

We should confess sin, whether only to God or also to the person we have offended, as soon as we recognize it. When it is impossible to talk to the person face to face, a phone call or letter will do.

But what if we have no way to get in touch with the person we have offended? One Sunday morning in Hong Kong, I was in church preparing my heart to take communion. Suddenly there flashed to mind an angry outburst against a fellow Christian three weeks earlier. I promptly asked the Lord to forgive me. But I wondered, "Should I take the Lord's Supper if I have not yet asked my brother's forgiveness?" I barely knew the man and had no idea how to get in touch with him. So I prayed, "Lord, I will make an effort to find him and will seek his forgiveness the first chance I get." I then felt free to eat the bread and drink the cup. As I left my seat after the service, I saw the man standing just ahead of me in the aisle. I went up to him, asked and received his forgiveness, and returned home thanking the Lord for His rapid help.

Always, if possible, we should settle accounts immediately, or before we go to bed at night.[17] When I refuse to admit my wrongness before going to sleep, I have a miserable night, tossing and turning and waking up frequently to review once again the reasons why I had a perfect right to act the way I did. Generally before I have finished my quiet time the next morning, I come to the conclusion that regardless of the other person's fault, I must seek forgiveness. Having done this, I can enjoy the Lord, my family, and my day.

When asking forgiveness, I find it best not to point out how the other person may be wrong. I focus on *my* sin, on *my* need to be forgiven.

Enjoy Instant Forgiveness

When we confess our sins, we need not put ourselves under hours or days of probation until we *feel* forgiven. God's warm welcome always awaits us the moment we admit our sin. As we *believe* in God's instant forgiveness and cleansing, we can pray with confidence and a clean conscience.

At a conference some years ago, Dawson Trotman, the founder of The Navigators, spoke to a large group of pastors and missionaries. Later one of his staff pointed out that in his message he had made critical remarks about another Christian. The following day, just before he spoke, Daws publicly asked for forgiveness from his fellow Christian leaders. In the process he broke down in tears.

What a humiliating situation! How could God possibly use the message of a man who had been so wrong the day before?

But Daws believed in instant forgiveness, and proceeded to preach one of his most powerful messages, "The Need of the Hour," which is still widely used today in print and on tape. It is full of the freshness and power of God's Spirit.

So it can be with us. One minute after we confess, we are as clean as if we had never sinned. We are free to pray, to enjoy the Word of God, to witness with boldness. No further remorse or apologies, no minutes or hours of self-condemnation or self-imposed penance to regain God's favor. We are free by God's grace—

by His unmerited attitude of favor and acts of favor—which over-flows to us more and more. Yet it overflows in vain if we fail to take advantage of it or if we try to deserve it. God invites us to partake confidently and *freely* of His unmerited favor, as Paul exhorted his spiritual son Timothy to do: "Be strong in the grace that is in Christ Jesus."[18]

Enjoying God's gracious and instant forgiveness requires three simple responses:

- We must be *honest in acknowledging* our sin.
- We must be *quick in confessing* our sin to God and others.
- We must be *bold in accepting* forgiveness and cleansing by faith.

Abiding in Christ and being cleansed of sin form firm foundations for our praying. They keep us in touch with God so that at any moment we can come to Him boldly and secure His help. They keep us on the path of obedience where nothing hinders our access to Him.

> Therefore, brothers, since we have confidence to enter the Most Holy Place by the blood of Jesus . . . and since we have a great priest over the house of God . . . let us come near to God with a sincere heart and a sure faith, with hearts that have been purified from a guilty conscience.[19]

Personal Application

1. What truths most impressed me in this chapter?
2. What should I do about one of them?

NOTES   1. Proverbs 28:13.
2. Proverbs 28:13, NIV.
3. Psalm 66:18.
4. Isaiah 58.
5. Isaiah 59:1–2.
6. Isaiah 58:9.
7. 1 Peter 3:7.
8. Ephesians 5:22–33.
9. 1 John 1:9, NIV.
10. 2 Corinthians 5:21.
11. John 13:8, italics added.
12. John 13:10.
13. Matthew 5:23–24.
14. 1 Peter 5:5; James 4:6.
15. Matthew 18:15, *The Living Bible.*

16. Galatians 6:1–2.
17. Ephesians 4:26.
18. 2 Timothy 2:1.
19. Hebrews 10:19, 21, NIV, and 22, TEV.

The Three Conditions
of Prayer

> God's mercy seat is no mere stall
> by the roadside, where every
> careless passer-by may put out
> an easy hand to snatch
> any glittering blessing
> that catches his eye.
> —Phillips Brooks

We cannot come to God in prayer on our own terms. Though He is a merciful and generous ruler, He is also righteous and wise. Therefore He has given guidelines for prayer that enable Him to answer without compromising His character or our true well-being. He has established simple conditions that make our prayers acceptable and assure answers.

Depending on God's Word includes knowing and following these guidelines, not to earn answers but to adapt ourselves to the principles by which God orders the spiritual universe.

In the preceding chapter, we considered the twin foundations for victorious praying.

- Abiding in Christ
- Being cleansed from known sin

These principles are the soil that nourishes a fruitful prayer life. They enable us to live in vital fellowship with God, doing what is pleasing in His sight in our praying as well as in our living.

Then as we pray, we must abide by the three conditions God has given:

- Pray in Jesus' name.
- Pray in God's will.
- Pray in faith.

Pray in Jesus' name

"And whatever you ask in My name, that will I do, that the Father may be glorified in the Son. If you ask Me anything in My name, I will do it."[1] Jesus is not saying that we must voice the words *in Jesus' name* at the end of every prayer. We need not dash back into our room after a time of prayer and breathe a quick "in Jesus' name," thinking the whole time of prayer would have been wasted otherwise. *In Jesus' name* is not a code phrase that gets prayers granted if we say it and cancels them if we do not.

Praying in Jesus' name means coming to God in the merits of the One who paid for our sins and represents us in the courts of heaven. It means entering the corridors of supreme power not because of our service, our sincerity, or our worthiness, but because we belong to Christ.

Imagine a man sitting on the steps of the White House, dejected, when a young boy comes up and asks, "What's the matter, Mister?"

"Run along Sonny, and don't bother me. I've got big problems. I've been trying to see the President for days but I can't get an appointment. Now leave me alone."

"Maybe I can help you."

"You? What could you do?"

"Take my hand."

To the man's surprise, they walk up the steps of the White House, past the guards, down the hall, past the secretary, to a door with a sign, "President of the United States." Without bothering to knock, the boy opens the door and leads the man into the presence of the President.

"This man would like to see you Daddy."

It is not the man's family background or letters of reference that gain him an audience with the President. It is not a good education or stylish suit or large bank account. It is because he comes with the President's son, who has special privileges. The man comes not on his own merits, but on those of the son.

Nothing we are, nothing we have achieved, gives us access to God. Our fruitfulness, our faithful quiet times, our discipline, our loving helpfulness to others; none of these tip the scales in our favor. As long as we depend on them, we disqualify ourselves for effective praying. We can come only by depending on Christ's worthiness, His forgiveness, His unlimited access to God. We come in the merits of God's Son, who has special privileges.

How encouraging it is to know also that no failure or lack in my life in any way can hinder my coming to God in prayer. My inadequacies do not matter since I come in the merits of Jesus Christ. I may be struggling with impurity or dishonesty. I may feel depressed or angry. I may lament my lack of faith, my laziness, or my indifference. If I had to come in my own worthiness, I would be totally disqualified.

But in Jesus' name, I can come just as I am, honestly acknowledging the things that would disqualify me. Even if I feel rebellious, I can come if I will confess my rebelliousness and yield it to Him. If I am full of doubts, I can tell Him about my wavering faith. Whatever my condition, I am to bring my need to God, coming in Jesus' name, depending on my status as one of His chosen, forgiven ones. This gives me freedom to state my petitions with confidence. This is what it means to pray in Jesus' name.

Helmut Thielicke wrote,

> We do not come merely in our own name . . . who are *we*, we who are drunk with hope, plagued by fear, and undermined by doubt; how could *we* ever rise above this sea of madness, how could we ever break through the blockades in our life?—we come, not in our own name, but in the name of the Lord Jesus. We come in His name not only because He has commanded us to pray, but because through His death and resurrection He has made us children of His Father, and therefore has given us the right to speak as children.[2]

Pray in God's Will

First John 5:14 assures us that if we ask anything according to God's will, He hears us. His will sometimes seems complicated or unclear. But He reveals His will in His Word, so praying in His will means praying according to His Word.

Having God's Word and Spirit to guide us, we can pray in the light of what we understand to be His will. Even a young Christian can discover enough of God's will in small and large matters to pray with confidence. God makes special allowances when we are new Christians, often answering even childish and unrealistic prayers. But He expects us to make progress and not to remain children in understanding. We must continually seek fresh knowledge of God and His ways, not becoming stagnant through laziness or rebellion. He expects us to discover His will and to pray accordingly.

As a young follower of Christ, I needed guidance on whether to transfer from an engineering to a liberal arts major and begin preparing for full-time Christian service. For many months I was unwilling to consider the shift. I had long wanted to be an engineer. One night sitting under the stars on a rocky ledge beside beautiful Lake Tahoe in the California mountains, I shared my struggle with my pastor. With his encouragement, I prayed and settled the lordship issue, telling God that I was willing to do His will.

During the following months I began to abide in Christ in a new way and started intensive study and memorizing of God's Word. As I continued to pray and seek the Lord's will, it became clear that He wanted me to make the switch and trust Him for the results. Though I was young and immature in my spiritual life, God gave sufficient light and confidence for the decision. I prayed for guidance and ability in my new direction. The years since have confirmed that though I was spiritually young, He indeed showed me His will and fulfilled my requests.

But God wants us to mature. He expects continuing progress. In John 15:7 Christ says that if we maintain continuous fellowship with Him, and His words have a deep and controlling place in our lives and thinking, we can ask whatever we want and it will be done. This does not mean that we have to become spiritual giants before we can pray and receive answers. It does mean that we have to keep growing in knowledge and understanding. We must become more conformed to His revealed principles and plans, learning to see things from His point of view. Increasingly we must let God's Word and His indwelling Spirit keep us from sin and from asking with wrong motives. The more we know of His will and follow it, the more confident we become in prayer.

Pray in Faith

In *The Disciplines of Life*, V. Raymond Edman, former president of Wheaton College, wrote,

> To walk by faith is to face an unending succession of giants, Jordans, and Jerichos, and to conquer each one in turn. Whatever may be our Jericho, it will not jeer at us indefinitely if we obey the Word and will of God. Prayer and patience will bring it low before the soul that dares to obey God.[3]

Faith is the master key to our whole relationship with God. It is a major condition for answered prayer. "And everything you ask in prayer, believing, you shall receive."[4] "If you have faith as a mustard seed . . . nothing shall be impossible to you."[5] "Blessed is she that believed: for there shall be a performance of those things which were told her from the Lord."[6]

These are sweeping promises that depend only on God's unlimited power and on our faith. These promises are not made to the masses who are out of touch with God. They are not a magic formula to achieve selfish or foolish ends. Only in a cleansed, abiding life that seeks God's will and approaches God in Jesus' merits can genuine faith flourish. To such a person, Christ's promises offer the key to prayer that receives answers and accomplishes impossibilities, the key of faith.

But what is faith? It is confidence in God's statements. It is counting on Him to be who He says He is and to do what He says He will do. Faith is not a subjective impression or feeling. As expressed by Alexander R. Hay, "Faith is not a force that we exercise or a striving to believe that something shall be, thinking that if we believe hard enough it will come to pass."[7] Faith is an attitude of trust. It is putting confidence in objective reality, in God Himself and His Word. In *Letters to Malcolm*, C. S. Lewis warns,

We must not encourage in ourselves or others any tendency to work up a subjective state which, if we succeeded, we should describe as "faith," with the idea that this will somehow insure the granting of our prayer. We have probably done this as children. But the state of mind which desperate desire, working on a strong imagination, can manufacture is not faith in the Christian sense. It . . . is a feat of psychological gymnastics.[8]

Faith is simple trust. We see it in a child who trusts his mother to help him safely across a busy street, or one who jumps fearlessly from the stairs when his father promises to catch him.

Faith is a switch that connects the power of God with the need we bring to Him in prayer. The power lies not in our faith, but in God, even as the power to run a motor or light a lamp lies not in the switch but in the electricity.

Troubling Doubts. On its simplest level, praying in faith requires just enough confidence to look to the Lord and invite Him into the need that concerns us. At times all we have is a tiny-but-honest faith that says, "Lord, I believe; help my unbelief."[9] In such a prayer we honestly express our doubt, yet we choose to side with belief. We choose against the unbelief that is nibbling at the edges of our confidence, and we ask God to deliver us from it. As with the man who first uttered this prayer, the Lord accepts such a response as faith. This kind of faith, though attacked by unbelief, is far removed from the deliberately chosen position of unbelief mentioned in Matthew 13:58: "And He did not do many miracles there because of their unbelief." "Help-my-unbelief faith" is valid faith.

Faith takes different forms in different personalities. Some experience a high degree of certainty. Others encounter persistent intellectual doubts although their commitment to Christ is definite and they are growing spiritually. A settled, uncontested faith eludes them. Such people can honor God in a unique way by choosing to believe even though their faith is not reinforced by feelings of certainty.

Most of us experience times when we waver as we bring a need to the Lord in prayer, looking to Him one moment, looking at human impossibilities the next. Even the apostle Peter wavered

THE THREE CONDITIONS OF PRAYER

in his faith. Trusting Christ, he began to walk on the water.[10] Then, as he felt the force of the wind and saw the raging waves, doubt flooded his heart and he began to sink. But he corrected his error, once again fixing his faith on Jesus with the simple cry, "Lord save me!" Jesus immediately answered his prayer. We too must turn our eyes back to the Lord and His Word whenever uncertainty and doubt assault us.

Thoughts that Hinder Faith. Sometimes we weaken our faith by submerging ourselves in doubt-developing thoughts. Over and over we think, "Does God really care about me? Might things go better if I worked them out myself? Can I trust God, or will He withhold the best from me?" Cultivating such thoughts can suffocate our faith. How we handle these thoughts is crucial.

When a doubting thought arises within us, the solution is not to deny it or push it aside. Rather we can acknowledge the thought to God, choose not to let it dominate us, and substitute a thought that coincides with God's Word. Then we can pray in spite of unanswered questions.

One man whom I highly respect told how he has learned to live and pray by faith although intellectual questions are always ready to surface in his mind. He related a specific instance when doubt spontaneously arose in his mind as he thought about a promise of God. He said, "The thought came. 'I wish I believed that promise,' and I countered it with the thought, 'Of course, I believe it. I have already chosen to believe.' " Many questions remain unanswered in his mind, but he chooses to think thoughts consistent with his chosen alignment with God.

We can either allow doubting thoughts to keep us from prayer, or we can bring them to God, asking Him to give us understanding as we continue to walk with Him. We can pray that if anything within us is hindering our certainty, God will show us what it is and how to overcome it.

Sometimes God answers our questions directly through His Word or through other people. At other times, without an actual answer, He settles our hearts as our understanding of Him increases. The important thing is not to let our questions keep us from praying and from feeding on God's Word.

Double-minded Doubting. The apostle James warns us about

the kind of doubting that wipes out the effectiveness of prayer—double-minded doubting. Some of the scattered Christian Jews to whom he wrote did not receive answers from God because they asked out of selfish ambition, pride, and lust. Regardless of God's will, they wanted their craving satisfied. They listened to God's Word but refused to change their ways, resisting God though they posed as His friends. Their doubt was rooted in disobedience, in divided loyalties.[11] James warned that such a person could not expect answers to his prayers. A person who sincerely desires God's answer

> must ask in sincere faith without secret doubts as to whether he really wants God's help or not. The man who trusts God, but with inward reservations, is like a wave of the sea, carried forward by the wind one moment and driven back the next. That sort of man cannot hope to receive anything from God, and the life of a man of divided loyalty will reveal instability at every turn.[12]

The disobedient Christian cannot pray about any concerns in faith. If we find ourselves blown back and forth by this kind of doubting, we should change our request to "Search me, O God, and know my heart; Try me and know my anxious thoughts; And see if there be any hurtful way in me, And lead me in the everlasting way."[13]

Stable Faith. As our knowledge of God and His Word grows deeper, our faith becomes more stable. We become increasingly assured of God's will, His love, and His power. We go beyond a vague belief in God, grasping the idea that He deeply cares for us, that He wants to work on our behalf, and that nothing is difficult for Him. We become like Abraham, who knew God as the One who can call into being that which does not exist. After being told that his wife, Sarah, would have a child even though both she and Abraham were too old, "he did not waver in unbelief, but grew strong in faith, giving glory to God, and being fully assured that what He had promised, He was able also to perform."[14] In a situation that was far beyond the realm of human possibility, Abraham counted on the promise of God. Abraham's strong faith was rooted in God's promises, not in Abraham's personal desires.

In *Quiet Talks on Prayer*, S. D. Gordon points out how a stable faith develops:

> The faith that believes that God will do what you ask is not born in a hurry; it is not born in the dust of the street and the noise of the crowd. Its birthplace is in the secret place; and time, the open Word, and a reverent heart are necessary to its growth. Into that heart will come a simple strong faith that the thing it is led to ask shall be accomplished.[15]

General and Specific Faith. Praying with faith can take two forms, depending on how clearly we know God's will in the matter being considered.

Sometimes God does not give us clarity about the outcome He desires. Yet we can pray with a settled confidence that He is able to work, and will do so. We can commit our way to the Lord and trust Him to accomplish His good, pleasing and perfect will, even though we do not yet know the details or timing. Prayer opens the way for God to do what He wants, whether or not we know in advance what that is.

On one of my early trips through South Asia, fellow missionary Jim North and I visited an "impossible" city, a national religious center impervious to Christianity. After we trudged the streets and campus of this stronghold of Satan and conversed with students and townspeople, I commented, "Well, we might be able to start something here eventually, but it will take years."

So we prayed believing but with no special leading, asking God to enable us someday to raise up mature disciples and disciplemakers in that university and city.

God arranged an early answer. Within months two men from the city contacted me. One man, having had some exposure to The Navigators during his student days in America, phoned me on the only day in four months that I was at home in Singapore. The other man, a fiery young believer, sent me three letters and two telegrams urging me to visit him at the university during my next trip. Though he soon transferred to another city, he opened doors to medical and engineering students and to key couples, doors that have remained open for nine years. Some of those who received Christ have become foundations for a fruitful ministry among both Christians and non-Christians, an expanding ministry that continues to produce laborers.

Ten years ago we prayed with faith but without clarity on details or timing. God heard and worked. We did not need great faith, but ordinary faith in a great God.

At other times, when one has clearly discerned God's will, he can pray with a stronger, more settled faith. He should then be bold to request specifically what God has shown to be His will. This is the second form of praying in faith. Certain about what God wants, we ask with confidence that He will accomplish it.

When Ruth and I knew God was leading us to Singapore, we began praying for specific things that we felt were His will. Besides asking for the right place to live, guidance on the children's schooling, and empowering for our ministry opportunities, we specifically prayed for a good used car. God led us to make two requests—a car that would last for a long time, and a used one as the best use of His money.

Within a few days after arriving in Singapore, a friend poring over the want ads in the Straits Times spotted an unusually good buy: an almost-new Toyota offered at a twenty percent discount because the owner's company had given him a larger car. The Toyota proved to be outstanding for eight years—adequate for our needs and ministry, with exceptional gas economy and a minimum of rust and repairs. And we were able to sell it for almost the amount we had paid. We had specifically prayed in faith, and the Lord answered beyond our expectations.

George Mueller was the founder of orphan homes in Bristol, England, in the 1900s. He was a man of Christlikeness, depth in the Word, and aggressive evangelism. But he is best remembered for his remarkable faith and answers to prayer. He wrote,

> I have found invariably, in the fifty-four years and nine months through which I have been a believer, that if only I believed, I was sure to get in God's time the thing I asked for. . . . We must believe that God is able and willing. To see that He is able, you have only to look at the resurrection of the Lord Jesus Christ; for having raised Him from the dead, He must have almighty power. As to the love [and willingness] of God, you have only to look at the

cross of Christ. . . . With these proofs of the power and love of God, assuredly, if we believe, we shall receive—we shall obtain.[16]

Signposts for Answered Prayer

As we abide in Christ cleansed of known sin, observing the three conditions of prayer is simply part of our willing response to the Lord, often without conscious thought. The conditions are the outflow of our abiding, dependent relationship with Him rather than methods we use in order to qualify for answers. God didn't intend them to be a burdensome list of requirements piled on one another to make prayer difficult, or a checklist to use every time we pray.

Instead, He gave them as signposts for effective prayer. They can correct us when we rely on our human merits, preferences, or impressions. They can encourage us when confidence in our prayer-answering God wavers. When our prayers are unanswered, rather than feeling that God is unfaithful or that prayer is futile, we can review the foundations and conditions, asking God to keep us within these guidelines. We may only need to continue asking.

How gracious of our Lord to provide these simple foundations and conditions so that we can enjoy the privilege of answered prayer. Here they are again.

In our lives we are to
    abide in Christ;
    be cleansed of known sin.
In our praying we are to
    pray in Christ's name;
    pray in God's will;
    pray in faith.

The twin foundations of prayer, abiding and being cleansed, lead us into a relationship with God through which He can answer our prayers without acting contrary to His nature. They align us with His good plans for us and the world. The three conditions lead us further into this relationship, keeping us humble and dependent. Both the foundations and the conditions release us from our narrow thoughts and ambitions into the freedom and fullness of God, "who is able to do immeasurably more than all we ask or imagine, according to His power that is at work within us."[17] These foundations and conditions for prayer draw us into active partnership with God. Then as He hears and answers, our relationship with Him grows yet deeper.

Personal Application

1. Which one of the three conditions do I most need to strengthen? How?
2. What is one hindrance to my faith that I should pray about and work to remove?

NOTES
1. John 14:13–14.
2. Helmut Thielicke, "Talking About God or With God?" *Leadership*, summer 1980, page 51.
3. V. Raymond Edman, *The Disciplines of Life* (World Wide Publications, 1948), pages 30–31.
4. Matthew 21:22.
5. Matthew 17:20.
6. Luke 1:45, KJV.
7. Alexander R. Hay, as quoted in *Green Letters* by Miles Stanford (Zondervan Publishing House, 1975), page 12.
8. C. S. Lewis, *Letters to Malcolm: Chiefly on Prayer* (Harcourt Brace Jovanovitch, 1963), page 60.
9. Mark 9:24, KJV.
10. Matthew 14:22–33.
11. The double-mindedness of James 1:8 is described in James 3:13–4:10.
12. James 1:6–8, PH.
13. Psalm 139:23–24.
14. Romans 4:20–21.
15. S. D. Gordon, *Quiet Talks on Prayer* (Grosset & Dunlap, 1904), pages 158, 224–225, 158.
16. Robert Steer, *George Mueller: Delighted in God* (London: Hodder and Stoughton, 1975), page 265.
17. Ephesians 3:20, NIV.

Part II
A Pattern of Prayer

In the Gospels, Christ gives over one hundred examples, teachings, and exhortations about prayer. The Gospel of Luke is especially helpful, as is Luke's other book, Acts, which abounds in examples of praying. These two books give us more than one-fourth of the information on prayer in the New Testament.

Luke eleven contains Christ's greatest teaching on prayer. It has three notable sections:

- The Lord's prayer (verses one through four)
- Persistence in prayer (verses five through ten)
- Prayer for the Holy Spirit (verses eleven through thirteen)

In Part II we will analyze the rich pattern for prayer that Jesus taught His disciples, frequently titled "The Lord's Prayer" or "The Disciples' Prayer." Persistence in prayer and praying for the Holy Spirit will be covered in chapters seventeen and eighteen.

5

Thy Name, Thy Kingdom, Thy Will

[In the Lord's Prayer] Jesus laid
down principles governing
man's relationship to God . . . It
should be noted that He did not
say, "Pray these precise words,"
but, "Pray, then, in this way." He
was giving a pattern, not an
inflexible form.
—J. Oswald Sanders,
Prayer Power Unlimited

In Luke eleven Jesus gives His disciples the simple yet profound pattern for prayer that Matthew records in its slightly fuller form.

> Our Father who art in heaven,
>> Hallowed be Thy name.
>> Thy kingdom come.
>> Thy will be done,
>> On earth as it is in heaven.
>>> Give us this day our daily bread,
>>> And forgive us our debts, as we also have forgiven our debtors.
>>> And do not lead us into temptation, but deliver us from the evil one.
>> For Thine is the kingdom, and the power, and the glory, forever. Amen.[1]

In its major teachings and more subtle implications, this prayer is filled with lessons for our daily times of prayer. It provides a pattern, a framework, that we can fill in with our own thoughts and requests. As you read these chapters in Part II, mark ideas and portions you would like to use in your personal times with God.

The first three requests in this prayer highlight a major purpose of prayer—to glorify God. Consistent, effective prayer flows from a heart bent on honoring His name, advancing His kingdom, and doing His will.

Our Father Who Art in Heaven

Jesus instructs His followers to preface their requests with the words *our Father*. Because we have been born into His family through trusting Christ, the God to whom we come in prayer is truly our Father, eager to hear our voice. We can address Him as "Father" in the warm, familiar way a child says "Daddy." We do not come as cringing slaves to an austere master, but as God's own children, part of His intimate family circle. "You can say with a full heart, 'Father, my Father.' "[2]

When you say "our Father," do you realize what kind of Father He is? We are not calling on a father who is so preoccupied with his career that he has little time for his children, one who is a provider but little more. We are not calling on a father who may find someone else he loves more, and so forsake us. Nor does the Father to whom we pray indulgently cater to our whims or let us manipulate Him. He is not weak and passive, or unable to make decisions. He does not hold to the modern idea that submitting to His authority would warp His children's personalities, or rob them of their right to be themselves.

Instead we are calling on a strong and wise Father, One who knows that only by submitting to Him will we become the persons we were meant to be. He gives us the security of guidelines and limits. He does not force us to obey them, yet He expects us to do so and disciplines us if we do not. If we insist on willful independence, He lets us learn from the consequences and takes back the key to His storehouse. He does this not to dominate, but to liberate us. He does it so that we will again yield to His lordship and choose His good plan.

Our Father knows the number of hairs on our head and sees our every teardrop. His heart is filled with thoughts of good toward us more numerous than the grains of sand by the seashore. He is always available, always receptive to our prayers. He never changes his mind, never develops a do-not-disturb-Me attitude, and never goes on trips. Being infinite in love and capacity, He surpasses the best our minds can imagine in an ideal father. A. W. Tozer wrote,

> From a failure properly to understand God comes a world of unhappiness. . . . The Christian life is thought to be a glum, unrelieved cross carrying under the eye of a stern Father who expects much and excuses nothing. The truth is that God is the most winsome of all beings and His service one of unspeakable pleasure. He loves us for ourselves and values our love more than galaxies of new created worlds.[3]

The prayer continues, "Our Father *who art in heaven.*" The words translated "in heaven" literally mean "in the heavens." This means the highest heaven, where angels worship before God's throne. It also includes the other heavens referred to in the Bible— the vast reaches of space and the atmospheric heaven that surrounds us. As G. Campbell Morgan says, God dwells in "the heaven of the seraphim, the heaven of the stars, and the heaven of the sparrows."

Remembering that our affectionate Father is also the great and awesome sovereign of the universe, we must balance our familiarity with respect and reverence. We are humble, dependent beings as well as beloved children. Without His permission we could not draw our next breath. And were we not cleansed of all moral blots through the sacrifice of Christ, we would shrink in terror before His blazing purity. Yet he invites us to come boldly, addressing Him as "Father."

We can bring joy to our Father's heart by expressing our appreciation and our need of Him. Worship Him as you read the following prayer.

> Father, thank You for the wealth of love You have lavished upon me, that I should be Your child. I love You and deeply appreciate that You are strong, yet tenderly affectionate; You are exalted, yet personally involved with me. Thank You that You care enough to

establish guidelines and expect obedience. I bow before You as the great, majestic ruler of the universe, and acknowledge how weak and insignificant I am compared to You, how dependent I am on Your goodness and mercy, how far short I fall of Your glory, and how grateful I am for Your forgiveness and Your warm welcome!

Hallowed Be Thy Name

That God's name be hallowed (honored, kept holy) is the first of seven requests. "But is not His name eternally holy?" you ask. Yes, but He wants to make His name holy and honored *in people's eyes through us.* We should pray that in all our attitudes and actions, we will honor Him. We can also pray that people in all nations will honor His name. And we can honor His name through praise. Prayer that is based on passages of Scripture as a basis for our praise is a rewarding way to honor Him.

Splendid and majestic is Your work, holy and awesome is Your name. From the rising of the sun, even to its setting, Your name is great among the nations, You who are the trust of all the ends of the earth and of the farthest sea. You are exalted above all the peoples. Let them praise Your great and awesome name![4]

May all that is within me bless Your holy name and remember all Your benefits. May Your name be honored today through my thoughts and words, through my attitudes and reactions. I give You myself to be an instrument of Your righteousness and love and peace. Thank You for Your help in this.[5]

How right it is to begin with the request, "Hallowed be Thy name," for our entire prayer life should be backed by the desire to glorify God. O. Hallesby states that

if we will make use of prayer, not to wrest from God advantages for ourselves or for our dear ones, nor to escape from tribulations and difficulties, but to call down upon ourselves and others those things which will glorify the name of God, then we shall see the strongest and boldest promises of the Bible about prayer fulfilled also in our weak little prayer life.[6]

Thy Kingdom Come

The second petition, "Thy kingdom come," concerns the progress of God's kingdom, daily as well as when Jesus Christ returns to reign on earth. It requests His reign in the world *and* in our lives. It is hypocritical to pray "Thy kingdom come" if we are not submissive to the King. We might expand the request:

> Father, thank You that Your kingdom has come in my heart, that You have transferred me from Satan's power into the kingdom of Your dear Son. Help me today to advance the cause of Your kingdom. By contentment and faithfulness in my routine tasks; by loving service and by word, may I help Your kingdom to come in the lives of people around me, making them thirsty for You. And I eagerly look forward to the return of Your Son, to usher in Your kingdom in its fullness. Come quickly, Lord Jesus!

Why do we long for His return and pray for the establishment of His kingdom on earth? Isaiah 9:6–7 gives some reasons:

> And the government will rest on His shoulders;
> And His name will be called Wonderful Counselor, Mighty God,
> Eternal Father, Prince of Peace.
> There will be no end to the increase of His government or of peace,
> On the throne of David and over his kingdom,
> To establish it and to uphold it with justice and righteousness
> From then on and forevermore.

Alan Redpath reminds us that

> this world of ours has not been abandoned to the devil. It is yet to be the scene of the greatest triumph of God. This earth, which began with the miracle of creation, which has witnessed the miracle of the empty tomb, is once again to see the glory of God and experience the reign of Jesus Christ our Lord. This is the fulfillment for which we pray.[7]

We can enlarge this request by praying for people who are working for His kingdom where we live and throughout the world.

Thy Will Be Done

The next request in the Lord's Prayer is, "Thy will be done, on earth as it is in heaven." How is the will of God done in heaven? Constantly. Totally. And gladly. To pray "Thy will be done" commits us to active, unreserved cooperation with God. First it means, "May Your will be done by me, in my corner of the earth." Jesus teaches us to align ourselves with God's purposes, giving Him the chance to influence the world through our lives. In effect, we should pray, "Do what You want to in me and through me; and have Your way in my circumstances."

"Thy will be done" is not a passive request. It is not a resigned, "Whatever will be, will be." Knowing who God is and yielding to Him means joyful acceptance of His plans. Sometimes we fear that yielding to God will result in bitter trials and disasters. We say, "Your will be done" with resignations and doubts. Then He surprises us with blessings and deep satisfaction.

Besides praying that God's will be done in our lives, we should ask this for others both inside and outside the Kingdom—for fellow Christians and Christian workers, and for people they witness to. We should also pray for government leaders, asking that God will give them wisdom and courage, will lead them to make decisions that are just, and also helpful to the cause of Christ, or that He will overrule through circumstances. We can also pray that God will intervene in social, political, and economic situations so that the Gospel may advance. As Alan Redpath declares,

> Every time we breathe this prayer we touch upon the root of all human suffering and pray for its removal. . . . The Christian subject to the Holy Spirit and utterly submissive to the will of God is the mightiest factor in world revolution to bring about God's kingdom.[8]

Personal Application

1. What impressed me in this chapter about God, or about how to honor Him in my praying?
2. What do I plan to do about this?

NOTES   1. Matthew 6:9–13, including NASB marginal notes ("the evil one").
2. Romans 8:15, PH.

3. A. W. Tozer, *The Root of the Righteous* (Christian Publications, Inc., 1955), pages 14–15.
4. Based on Psalm 111:3 and 9, Malachi 1:11, Psalm 65:5, and 99:2–3.
5. Based on Psalm 103:1–2.
6. O. Hallesby, *Prayer* (England: InterVarsity Press), page 105.
7. Alan Redpath, *Victorious Prayer* (Fleming H. Revell Company, 1957), pages 55–56.
8. Redpath, pages 53 and 59.

6

Our Daily Bread

Prayer fulfills the Master's ideal
only when it begins with the
interests of God and follows with
the needs of man.
—G. Campbell Morgan,
The Practice of Prayer

The first three requests of the Lord's Prayer focus on God and His eternal interests. The last four requests concern our human needs.

Our Daily Bread

"Give us today the food we need."[1] Here is the divine precedent for praying about our physical necessities. God is personally concerned about the daily needs of His children, as emphasized by Dr. Howard Hansen: "Here is one of the great and continuing needs—to sustain the life of the body and minister to its health and strength ... Prayer is not something that is limited to the wild blue yonder. Prayer is something that can affect our lives upon a very solid earth."

"Bread" means "food," but also applies to other material and practical concerns of our lives, such as clothing and housing. Out of His glorious abundance in Christ Jesus, God promises to supply all our necessities—not all our wants, but all our needs. Having to pray for our needs day by day helps to keep us in continual dependence upon Him.

Notice that this request follows the ones centering on God's interests: *His* name, *His* kingdom, and *His* will. To those who put God's interests first Jesus promises, "All these things will be given to you as well."[2] A good friend frequently comments, "My wife and I have decided to avoid the phrase *We can't afford it*. If we don't have the money for something, it is not God's will or not His time for us to have it."

Poor or Affluent

Many people in our world go hungry unless they pray for and receive special provisions for "today." To be in need gives us the opportunity to pray and trust God, and to experience the thrill of receiving material provisions through prayer.

Strangely, the affluent as well as the poor have anxieties about material and financial security. When we have plenty, we can well pray,

> Lord, I realize that You continually provide for me. My food, my clothing, my shelter—all come from You. Thank You for Your supply! Enable me to put You first, so that I can rest on Your promise that my needs will always be provided for even in financial loss or economic disaster. Enable me to be generous so that I will enjoy Your liberality both materially and spiritually.[3]

Whatever our financial status, we have physical needs we can bring before our Father. We can pray daily for health and strength. We can pray, "Lord, enable us to get a real bargain on the car we need, and what we save we will use for You." We can pray about finding the right job, an anticipated cut in pay, and that unexpected medical bill that our income will not cover.

One November when Ruth was a widow, a thyroid operation depleted her bank account. As December began, she and the children sat at the dining room table praying about their needs. Her daughter, Doreen, thanked God for His many past provisions; Ruth presented several requests; and her son, Brian, thanked the Lord in advance for the way He was going to answer. That month God provided for the medical bills and all other expenses plus another gift designated "for something special for Christmas," which was another answer to prayer.

Families that have specific financial needs have a great opportunity as they pray for their daily bread. When he was in high school, Brian saw God repeatedly provide for his family in answer to prayer. He commented, "Mom, I'm not sure God answers my prayer, but I know He answers yours." This knowledge helped prepare him to trust God for answers to his own prayers.

Because of frequent moves to strange cities and countries, we have often prayed for housing, using Deuteronomy 1:32–33: "The Lord your God ... goes before you on your way, to seek out a place for you to encamp." We begin praying as far ahead of the planned move as possible, and the Lord often provides in exciting ways. Our most recent needs have been for housing during furloughs in the States. Once God provided a fully furnished home in Ames, Iowa, vacated for exactly the five months we needed it by an elderly couple escaping from the icy Midwest to Florida. On our next furlough, Ruth's brother Jake let us live in a rental home he owned. The week we needed to move in, the house unexpectedly became available because the tenants broke their lease and moved out.

Inner Resources

"Daily bread" in the Lord's Prayer refers to physical needs, but we can make the same request for our spiritual and emotional needs. When Jesus said, "I am the bread of life," He meant that He could satisfy our inner needs.[4] In Christ we have all the resources we need to live obedient, abundant lives. We can pray, "Lord, today enable me to partake of You as my bread of life. Be to me what I need for my hungers and thirsts, my responsibilities, and my relationships."

Bernard of Clairveaux, in his twelfth century hymn, wrote of the joy of feeding on Christ:

> We taste Thee, O Thou living Bread,
> And long to feast upon Thee still.
> We drink of Thee, the Fountainhead,
> And thirst our souls from Thee to fill.

In praying for our daily bread, we humble ourselves before God, admitting our dependence on Him for every detail of our lives. This opens us to His grace for both material and spiritual needs, for He opposes the proud but gives abundant grace to the humble.[5]

Personal Application
1. Prayerfully review this chapter and list two or three physical or spiritual needs you want to pray about.
2. Select one of those needs and pray about it until the Lord answers.

NOTES   1. Matthew 6:11, TEV.
          2. Matthew 6:33, NIV.
          3. Based on Proverbs 11:24–25, 19:17, Matthew 6:31–33, and 2 Corinthians 9:6–11.
          4. John 6:35.
          5. James 4:6.

7

Forgive Us Our Sins

> *I could dismiss half my patients tomorrow if they could be assured of forgiveness.*
> —head of a large British hospital

"Forgive us our debts, as we also have forgiven our debtors," we read in Matthew's account of the Lord's Prayer.[1] Luke explains more clearly the kind of debts we are to forgive—those owed not to the bank or the landlord, but to God: "Forgive us our *sins*, for we also forgive everyone who sins against us."[2]

All our sins—past, present, and future—were borne by Christ on the cross. When we trusted Him, He removed forever our guilt before our holy God, and He never places it back on us. "What joy there is for anyone whose sins are no longer counted against him by the Lord."[3] Though our sins as believers weigh on our consciences and prevent intimacy with our Father until we confess, they never return us to a position of guilt and enmity in God's sight. We are completely free from their penalty. Because we have been totally forgiven, God wants us to be forgiving.

Forgive Us as We Forgive Others

For many years I wrestled with the connection between the two parts of this request—God's forgiveness and ours. Does He forgive us only if we forgive others? Is not His forgiveness dependent solely on Christ's payment? In this request, Jesus is dealing with a forgiving *attitude*. Is my heart tender and responsive to the Spirit when relating to others, or resentful and unforgiving, hard and demanding? An unforgiving spirit damages my fellowship with God and hinders my prayers.

If I come to God asking for forgiveness yet am not willing to forgive another, I am saying, "Lord, forgive the particular sin I've mentioned, but overlook the grudge and bitterness I am holding onto." God says, "No, before you can sincerely ask to be cleansed, you must forgive that person who has failed or offended you." It is not that God is reluctant to forgive. Forgiveness is always flowing from His heart. He is always eager to welcome us back into full friendship with Himself. I may, however, ask God's forgiveness with my mouth, yet by my unforgiving spirit lock the door and prevent forgiveness from entering my experience. Or my negative attitude may blind me to my need of cleansing, so that I do not even ask for forgiveness.

Failure to forgive eats away my spiritual health just as termites destroy a house. In Matthew 18 Jesus told the parable of a man who was forgiven a debt equaling millions of dollars, then refused to forgive an insignificant debt worth a few hundred dollars. As a result, his master had him punished until he repaid the millions he owed.

Applying the story, Jesus said, "So shall My heavenly Father also do to you, if each of you does not forgive his brother *from your heart*."[4] How many of us suffer in mind and heart, perhaps even in body, because we have not forgiven someone? It may be the pain of our anger or resentment that consumes us like a corrosive acid. It may be the torment of self-condemnation because we are disobeying God's command, "You shall love your neighbor as yourself."[5] It may be the anguish of inner conflicts and spiritual emptiness. The only way to *enjoy* God's forgiveness and love is to forgive from the heart the person who offended us. Dr. Howard Hansen helps us understand why we should forgive:

> Jesus is not teaching that the *price* of our forgiveness with God is
> that we forgive our fellow men . . . Neither is Jesus teaching that all

we need to do to get the forgiveness of God is to be forgiving, and if we forgive our fellow men, then we place an obligation upon the Almighty to forgive us . . . God's forgiveness is not simply an echo of our own spirit of forgiveness. It is rather the other way around—the thought of the greatness of God's forgiveness . . . should rebuke us and mellow our hearts to such an extent that we would be willing to forgive others.

God's Forgiveness
What if God *did* forgive us only in the same way and to the same degree that we forgive others? We would be in deep trouble. He knows all our thoughts, our private words, our secret actions. Were He as demanding of us as we are with others, we would be without hope. "Lord, if You keep in mind our sins then who can ever get an answer to his prayers? But You forgive! What an awesome thing this is!"[6]

Fortunately God's forgiveness surpasses ours as the universe surpasses our tiny earth. He forgives not only our conscious sins of action and inaction, but even our hidden faults.[7] He instantly forgives and eternally forgets. He does not expect our forgiveness to match the perfection of His, but He does expect us to be quick to forgive, and to grow in our capacity to do so.

What if I confess my unforgiving spirit, yet the tentacles of resentment still clutch at my heart? The best cure is to meditate on the terrible, crushing weight of my sin that Jesus bore on the Cross, and the forgiving mercy of God in cancelling my immense debt and welcoming me into His family. I can let Christ's Spirit soften my heart with these truths, then by His power choose to obey Ephesians 4:32—"Be kind to one another, tender-hearted, forgiving each other, just as God in Christ also has forgiven you." When any hint of resentment lingers, I can ask for the Holy Spirit to remove it and replace it with the love of Christ. Lord Herbert stated it well: "He who cannot forgive others breaks the bridge over which he himself must pass."[8]

Sins of Neglect
Asking forgiveness goes beyond confessing actual wrongdoings. We are also to confess our failures and neglects. It is not enough

to say, "Lord, I haven't done anything very bad." We should also ask, "Have I done all that I ought to do?" Because God holds us responsible not only to avoid wrong actions and attitudes but also to develop right ones, lack of obedient action or inner response incurs a debt of omission, something we owe and have not paid.

What do we owe God? We owe Him our undivided love. We owe Him the continual sacrifice of praise and thanksgiving. We owe Him our bodies as instruments for His use. We all fall short of letting our entire lives revolve around Him. How great is the debt we owe Him! How great are the debts we owe others: love, kindness, patience, and concern for their good above our own. We need to pray, "Forgive us our sins."

The recognition of our sins of omission as well as those of commission should humble us. The wonder of His unreserved forgiveness should stir us to express our gratefulness. "For Thou, Lord, art good, and ready to forgive, and abundant in lovingkindness to all who call upon Thee."[9]

As we ask the Lord to forgive our sins, our heart attitude should be like that expressed in the following prayer:

> Lord, I want to have a clean conscience, and I want to keep right, both with You and with people. I want to stay out of my old ruts, out of my muddy detours, and walk in close fellowship with You on "the highway of holiness."[10]

Personal Application
1. Do I have an unforgiving spirit toward anyone, or is there some other unconfessed sin in my life?
2. What should I do about this, and when do I plan to do it?

NOTES
1. Matthew 6:12.
2. Luke 11:4, NIV.
3. Romans 4:8, *The Living Bible.*
4. Matthew 18:35.
5. Galatians 5:14.
6. Psalm 130:3–4, *The Living Bible.*
7. Psalm 19:14.
8. Lord Herbert, as quoted by John MacArthur Jr. in *Jesus' Pattern of Prayer* (Moody Press, 1981), page 131.
9. Psalm 86:5.
10. Isaiah 35:8.

8

Deliver Us

*I want a principle within
Of watchful, godly fear,
A sensitivity to sin,
A pain to feel it near.*

*Help me the first approach to feel
Of pride or wrong desire,
To catch the wandering of the will,
And quench the kindling fire.*
—Charles Wesley

Do Not Lead Us into Temptation

The word *temptation* in the New Testament can mean an entice-ment to sin or a testing (a difficulty or problem). God permits testings to come for our development, but He never tempts us to sin. Enticements to sin come from Satan, the world, and our own evil inclinations.

Although God does not tempt us to sin, neither does He isolate us from dangers and difficulties. And temptations to sin accompany every testing He permits in our lives—temptations such as insisting on our own solutions, or simply not trusting Him. Both God and Satan have purposes in our trials. J. Oswald Sanders tells us what the aims of each are:

> God subjects His children to testing to eliminate the dross from the
> gold in their characters and to strengthen and establish them in
> holiness. The devil tempts in order to induce them to fall into sin.[1]

God wants to strengthen and remold us. Satan wants to lead us away from God into distrust, discouragement, and disobedience.

55

He seeks to exploit even our spiritual successes, tempting us to be proud or complacent.

This sixth request is similar to Christ's command in Matthew 26:41—"Watch and pray so that you will not fall into temptation. The spirit is willing, but the body is weak."[2] We are not to pray for a life without testings, but rather for the Father's protection and deliverance from enticements to sin. So in this request we are saying, "Lord, lead me. Steer me away from temptations to sin and from paths that would lead to sin—to either wrong action or lack of right action on my part."

God promises that He will never let us be tested, or tempted, beyond our strength to endure, but that He will always provide a way out.[3] So we can pray gratefully, "Thank You that You are the Sovereign, behind-the-scenes Controller of my situations, setting limits to my trials and preparing a way to escape temptation." Then when tested or tempted, we must look for the safety exit He provides, *and use it.*

God commands us to flee youthful lusts, to guard our thoughts with diligence, and to avoid friendships that will lead us astray. "Do not be deceived: 'Bad company corrupts good morals.' "[4] We are not to see how far we can go and still be safe, but how close we can keep to the Lord. So in this request about temptations, we affirm our desire to avoid evil. We tell God we do not want to toy with temptations; we do not want to swim at the brink of the waterfall. We ask Him to direct us away from "innocent" beginnings that would lead to sin. We ask for His help in becoming more like Jesus, who though tempted as we are, never yielded to sin. He always came through victorious, and that is what He wants for us.

Deliver Us from the Evil One

This last request relates to the preceding one but includes more—deliverance from the evil one himself. Satan does more than tempt God's children. The name Satan means "the opposer" or "the adversary." As the bitter opponent of the Trinity, he is also the ruthless enemy of each person who has been transferred from his power into God's kingdom. We must pray to be delivered from his attacks.

Before I trusted Christ, I asked the Air Force friend who was witnessing to me, "Why is Satan so malicious and vindictive against people, especially Christians? What good does it do him? If his ultimate doom is hell anyway, why is he so eager to get others to join him?"

My friend answered, "That is just the kind of being he is."

By nature Satan is an evil, supernatural rebel, a liar, and a murderer. He is powerful and crafty. He seeks to lure us into sin, excesses, false doctrine, and occult practices. He seeks to hinder our service for Christ. He accuses and condemns us, trying to blind us to the fact that "the Judge Himself has declared us free from sin."[5] Satan's passionate obsession is to discredit the Lord Jesus Christ, and he often attacks Him by attacking us.

Satan is too mighty for us to resist alone, but we can defeat him through the Word and prayer. We must ask our invincible Father to deliver us from Satan. And deliver us He will, if our heart commitment is, "Thy will be done."

The apostle Peter exhorts, "Be self-controlled and alert. Your enemy the devil prowls around like a roaring lion looking for someone to devour. Resist him, standing firm in the faith"[6] We must be watchful against Satan. We dare not become involved in or experiment with any of his evil ways or teachings. God was with Daniel when he was thrown into the lion's den, but Daniel had not entered the den to test God's power or to flirt with danger.

Defensive Prayer

The first three requests in the Lord's Prayer are concerned with God: His name, His kingdom, and His will. The fourth and fifth requests cover our daily needs for food and forgiveness. These last two teach us to pray against sin and Satan. Thus two of the seven requests are defensive prayers. Praying defensively is important.

How often do you pray defensively? I was first alerted to defensive praying by Dr. Robert Munger, whose example, prayers, and ministry have greatly contributed to my life. Through the years I have found it a safeguard to pray about things that I do not want to happen—things that would tarnish the Lord's glory or damage me spiritually.

If you were Satan, how would you scheme against yourself?

Where are your weak points? Where would you aim? When you consider how he could tempt you, what flashes to mind? Lust? Pride? Self-pity? Prayerlessness? A domineering spirit? An over-dependence on people? An undue need to control? Bitterness directed against God or others? Dishonesty? Spiritual coldness? These are some of the works of the flesh that both young and mature Christians must fight against.

Dr. Billy Graham prays against at least three things: wrong involvement with women, love of money, and pride. On the last point, Dr. Graham often quotes Isaiah 42:8—"I will not give My glory to another."

Dawson Trotman prayed against these three and included a fourth, "a critical spirit and tongue."

Often I pray against being sidetracked through wrong doctrine and spiritual coldness. Here's my defensive prayer list.

Lust or wrong involvement with women
Covetousness or possession-centeredness
Pride
A *critical spirit* and tongue
Wrong doctrine
Spiritual coldness

Ruth includes many of these in her defensive praying, but she also adds anxiety, self-reliance, and fear of disapproval.

Jot down the major areas where Satan could tempt you, and pray regularly against these temptations. Your list does not have to be exhaustive. Keep it brief, and use it. If you and I can figure out our weaknesses, so can Satan. He is at least as smart as we are. So we must pray defensively.

Stop and pray about one of the things mentioned above: "Lord, please keep me from being tempted by this. Thwart Satan's attacks. Give me strength to resist Satan and his counterfeit pleasures. Help me to choose Your way and Your pleasures, not his."

NOTES   1. J. Oswald Sanders, *Prayer Power Unlimited* (Moody Press, 1977), page 112.
        2. NIV.
        3. 1 Corinthians 10:13.
        4. 1 Corinthians 15:33.
        5. Romans 8:33, PH.
        6. 1 Peter 5:8–9, NIV.

9

The Kingdom, the Power, and the Glory

> Here I stand on the edge of an
> ocean of truth. I have picked up
> a few grains of sand, but the
> whole ocean lies beyond me,
> unknown.
> —Isaac Newton

Concluding Praise

"For Thine is the kingdom, and the power, and the glory, forever. Amen." Whether or not this concluding sentence is in your version of the Bible, it is a fitting climax to this inexhaustibly rich prayer. One of many Scripture passages that echo this majestic conclusion is 1 Chronicles 29:11–13—

> "Yours, O Lord, is the greatness and the power
> and the glory and the majesty and the splendor,
> for everything in heaven and earth is Yours.
> Yours, O Lord, is the Kingdom;
> You are exalted as head over all.
> Wealth and honor come from You;
> You are the ruler of all things. . . .
> Now, our God, we give You thanks,
> and praise Your glorious name."[1]

Ending our times of prayer with such an affirmation of God's greatness is exhilarating.

His is the kingdom. He is King of all kings. He now reigns over a boundless spiritual kingdom, having a position infinitely superior to any earthly ruler. The day will come when He will rule visibly over the entire world. As we praise Him for this, we acknowledge that we are His yielded subjects.

His is the power. All authority in the physical universe and on the earth is His. He created the galaxies and controls them, and in His time He will terminate them. He also controls the spiritual universe, and there is nothing in our life or situations which He cannot control. Nothing is hard or impossible for Him.[2] For this we give Him thanks.

His is the glory as the brilliantly majestic One, the Ancient of Days—the almighty God sent down to save, and coming back to judge. We can worship Him as the God of glory—a glory one day to be shared by us. Daniel witnessed that glory in a vision and recorded what he saw: "His clothing was white as snow, His hair like whitest wool. He sat upon a fiery throne brought in on flaming wheels, and a river of fire flowed from before Him. Millions of angels ministered to Him and hundreds of millions of people stood before Him."[3]

Brevity in Prayer

There is still more to be learned from this great prayer. Have you noticed how quickly these seven short, specific requests can be made? If you time yourself, you will discover that the whole prayer can be quoted thoughtfully in about twenty seconds.

Although Christ probably taught this prayer many times in His ministry, the first time it must have come as a surprise to the disciples. Having asked Jesus to teach them to pray, they probably expected an extended lesson. But the instruction was short. A modern listener would hardly have had time to take out his pen and notebook before Christ finished. The disciples undoubtedly found the richness of the prayer impressive, as we do. But its brevity also catches our attention. Seven requests in twenty seconds. At that pace we could make twenty-one requests a minute. We could communicate a great deal to God in a short time.

"Oh, but Christ doesn't want us to do that," some say. "You can't pray that way." The Lord may not lead you to use such concise requests, but He gives many the freedom to do so. It is liberating to realize that God accepts short requests as well as long ones, and that both are scriptural. Neither way is always best. We must let His Spirit guide our praying each time we enter His presence. But keep in mind that short requests are a valid way to pray, taught and practiced by the Lord Jesus Himself.

In brief prayers I often use a short biblical thought or phrase as my initial request for each person I pray for, expanding it as the Holy Spirit leads. I have used prayers such as, "Lord, give Rich and Helen a deep love for one another," and "Lord, help Dick and Jo to seek Your face, behold Your beauty, experience Your joy, and be effective." Sometimes I begin with a more detailed prayer: "Lord, help Brian to be deep in Your Word and prayer, delivered from temptation, Spirit-controlled, and effective in ministry." God understands even briefer requests such as, "Father, help Raja to be deep, delivered, effective, and healthy." I enjoy using such starters for those on my prayer list, then asking other things that the Lord brings to mind.

Dawson Trotman used to comment that in ordering a hamburger we don't have to say, "Take a hamburger patty, cook it on both sides, put it on a bun, add onions, catsup, mustard, pickles, and a little lettuce, wrap it, and hand it to me." We can say just, "Hamburger with the works, to go." Today we can be even briefer—just "Big Mac," or "Whopper."

Not only are the requests in the Lord's Prayer brief, they are simple as well. In his book *Victorious Praying* Alan Redpath highlights the simplicity of the prayer: "It is indeed so simple that a little child can understand it, yet so profound that its depths are unfathomable . . . Maybe the problem with many of us is that we have ceased to be children in our prayer life and we make it too complicated."[4]

Prayer Involves Words

Another truth that stands out in the Lord's Prayer is that Jesus taught His disciples to pray with words, as He Himself did in His great prayer in John 17. Wordless silence and listening are valid aspects of fellowship with Him, but we should couple our silence with verbal prayer. Jacques Ellul warns against prayer that "remains unarticulated, very ardent perhaps, but without content . . . the plunge into the vast silence, into the ineffable, into the incommunicable." Such praying resembles Hindu mysticism more than scriptural prayer.[5] God generally communicates to us with words, and He wants us to express our thoughts to Him in words. Our mind will wander and we will do little real praying if we do not phrase our prayers in words, at least mentally.

What rich and practical concepts the Lord included in this prayer, the most well-known and widely used of Scripture prayers. It is a matchless pattern. We can use its requests to stimulate our worship and for specific praying about our own lives, the lives of others, and God's purposes in the world.

Take a few moments now and pray this prayer, amplifying each request with your own personal thoughts and specific needs.

> Our Father who art in heaven,
>> Hallowed be Thy name,
>> Thy kingdom come.
>> Thy will be done,
>> On earth as it is in heaven.
>>> Give us this day our daily bread.
>>> And forgive us our debts, as we also have forgiven our debtors.
>>> And do not lead us into temptation, but deliver us from the evil one.
>> For thine is the kingdom, and the power, and the glory, forever.
>> Amen.

NOTES
1. NIV.
2. Luke 1:37.
3. Daniel 7:9–10, *The Living Bible.*
4. Alan Redpath, *Victorious Praying* (Fleming H. Revell, 1957), page 16.
5. Jacques Ellul, *Prayer and Modern Man* (The Seabury Press, 1970), pages 96–97.

PART III
The Practice of Prayer

We have considered principles and conditions of prayer in Part I, and the pattern of the Lord's Prayer in Part II.

In Part III we will cover practical suggestions for developing our prayer lives.

10

Keeping a Quiet Time

> Cause me to hear thy
> lovingkindness in the morning,
> for in thee do I trust; cause me to
> know the way wherein I should
> walk; for I lift up my soul unto
> thee. . . . Teach me to do thy will,
> for thou art my God.
> (Psalm 143:8–10, KJV)

Some years ago Lorne Sanny, president of The Navigators, asked the godly T. J. Bach, "Dr. Bach, in the many years that you have walked with the Lord, do you find it gets easier or harder to keep a daily quiet time?"

Dr. Bach replied, "Well, Brother Sanny, I find that we generally *make* time for the things that we think are most important." His answer reflects the fact that it does not necessarily become easier or harder to spend time with the Lord. It is a matter of choice and discipline.

How to Have a Quiet Time

Your daily quiet time, whether 15 or 100 minutes long, should include two things, the Word of God and prayer, with approximately half the time given to each. If you major in the Bible itself rather than devotional books, the benefit will be notably greater.

S. D. Gordon, in his books on prayer, repeatedly emphasized that God's Word must be the basis of all our praying because God Himself speaks in it. Gordon wrote that the Bible is a book, yet more than a book. He believed there is a living Presence in it that we should listen to. He described Bible reading as the listening side of prayer. If the ear-side of prayer was right, the tongue-side would be right. As we let God teach us through His Word, both our living and our praying become a response to what He says.

For the first year or two after I trusted Christ, I read a chapter a day in the New Testament. But sometimes I would finish a chapter and wonder what I had gotten out of it.

Now three things help me profit more from my daily time with God. First I begin with prayer: "Father, I need Your guidance and help today. Speak to me through Your Word. Help me to understand and obey." That's enough, though sometimes I pray longer. At times I pray the verses quoted at the beginning of this chapter, or the words of the song,

> Speak, Lord, in the stillness
> While I wait on Thee.
> Hush my heart to listen
> In expectancy.
> Speak, O blessed Master,
> In this quiet hour,
> Let me hear Your voice, Lord,
> And feel Your touch of power.

Second, I mark my Bible with a pencil or pen. To me, a well-marked Bible is comfortable and enjoyable, and marking helps me concentrate and remember highlights. I have experimented with complicated marking and color schemes, but I now find a red or blue ball point pen the most satisfactory. I underline words and phrases that stand out to me or draw a line next to a long passage.

Third, as I read through the Bible I choose a favorite verse each day from the passage I read, and mark a small "FV" in the margin. When three or four verses seem equally good, I weigh them prayerfully and choose one. This review and forced selection stimulates my meditation on the Word.

Even new believers find this plan helpful. Recently in South Asia, a Hindu just one day old in the Lord surprised me by picking Philippians 1:20 as his favorite verse: "I eagerly expect and hope that I will in no way be ashamed, but will have sufficient courage so that now as always Christ will be exalted in my body, whether by life or by death" (NIV).

How to Use Quiet Time Verses in Prayer

After picking my favorite verse, I ask God to teach me more about the verse and to help me put the truth to work in my life. I then use the verse in prayer for myself and for most of those on my prayer list. At other times I use my favorite verse as a basis for a short written prayer, which I pray for myself and others.

One day I picked Philippians 1:9 as my favorite verse: "And this I pray, that your love may abound still more and more in real knowledge and all discernment." Then I wrote this prayer: "Lord, help me to be more loving to others and also more discerning in little and big things." As I prayed this for myself, I included several relationships in which I lacked love or discernment. As I then prayed it for my wife, other needs came to mind. The same was true when I prayed it for my children, my pastor, a colaborer, and a man I had recently led to the Lord. My favorite verse became a basis for praying, and I included other requests as the Holy Spirit led.

In reading Philippians 2, I chose verses fourteen and fifteen and wrote, "Dear God, help me today not to argue or complain. Help me to shine for You and to share You with someone."

In Philippians 3, verse ten was my favorite, and I wrote, "Father, help me to be diligent in learning of Your Son, and to know Him more and more intimately."

Using your favorite verse as a basis for your quiet time praying will help fix it in your mind for further meditation and prayer throughout the day, and you will not need to wonder whether you profited from your morning's reading.

The favorite-verse approach is excellent for teaching a new believer to read the Bible. Since he is not deciding which verse is most important but merely which one he likes best, he needs no special background or ability. When I do this with another person, whether spiritually young or old, I briefly pray aloud for the Lord to teach us. Then we silently read the chapter and choose our favorite verses. Next we each mention the verse we picked and why we liked it. Finally we pray our verse for ourselves, for each other, and for others. To keep it simple, I prefer not to share other insights from the chapter until we have finished our sample quiet time. Then as we have time, we discuss further blessings, cross references, or important truths.

When travelling in Burma, my wife and I stayed with an Englishman I had led to Christ some months before. After he and I had a sample quiet time before breakfast, he said, "Isn't that a nice way to read the Bible!" He had been reading it daily, but merely as a history book. For him to expect personal fellowship with God and light through a particular verse was a delightful new idea. His response reminded me not to assume that even well-educated or established Christians know how to feed on God's Word or pray. People appreciate being shown *how* to have a quiet time, how to pray, how to witness.

Include Praise

Sometimes our quiet times may fit the following description found in *Quiet Time:* "We are burdened with requests—business that must be put through, guidance we need here, help there, petitions on behalf of this one or that. All important, all urgent, all worthy, but—just business after all."[1]

God loves to have us come to Him with our burdens and our business, but He also wants to hear our words of love and worship. A. W. Tozer wrote, "We are called to an everlasting preoccupation with God."[2] Perhaps your favorite verse will lead you to praise Him and tell Him how much you appreciate Him. When it does not, you can use another verse or a song to encourage grateful praise. Expressions of adoration and thanksgiving bring joy to the Lord's heart and help you to know Him better and love Him more.

To enrich your praise, find verses about Him that you especially like, and use them often. Here are four of my favorites:

> Great is the Lord, and highly to be praised;
> And His greatness is unsearchable. (Psalm 145:3)

> Who is like Thee among the gods, O Lord?
> Who is like Thee, majestic in holiness,
> Awesome in praises, working wonders? (Exodus 15:11)

> The Lord is righteous in all His ways,
> And kind in all His deeds.
> The Lord is near to all who call upon Him,
>   To all who call upon Him in truth.
> He will fulfill the desire of those who fear Him. (Psalm 145:17-19)

> Praise the Lord, O my soul;
>   all my inmost being, praise His holy name.
> Praise the Lord, O my soul, and forget not all His benefits.
> He forgives all my sins . . .
> He satisfies my desires with good things,
>   so that my youth is renewed like the eagle's.
>   (Psalm 103:1-5, NIV)

Daily Fellowship with the King

In the Bible, God's great men had one thing in common: they spent time alone with God, getting to know Him better. Daniel was prime minister of an empire, yet "three times a day he got down on his knees and prayed, giving thanks to his God."[3] Moses, responsible for leading two million Jews on a forty–year journey through the Sinai Desert, gained wisdom and strength through time in God's presence, as friend with friend. David, famous warrior and king, loved to spend time with God. We can read his quiet time diary in the Psalms.

The Lord Jesus is the greatest example. Isaiah's prophecy of Christ's coming shows that Jesus spent time alone with the Father regularly: "The Sovereign Lord has given me an instructed tongue, to know the word that sustains the weary. He wakens me morning by morning, wakens my ear to listen like one being taught."[4] We read in Mark 1:35 that during His earthly ministry He rose early in the morning while it was still dark, and went out to an isolated place to pray.

Why is the quiet time indispensable? Because the King of the universe wants to reveal Himself and His love to us daily. He wants to make us spiritually strong, joyful, and wise. He wants to give us light and guidance for the day so that its hours will satisfy us and contribute to His good purpose for our lives. He wants to arm us in advance against temptation and send us on our way with a song in our hearts and an appropriate word for the people we meet.

Left to ourselves, we fail to distinguish God's way from the world's, or we see the difference but give in to the world anyway. We may have an uneasy feeling but rationalize our actions by saying, "After all, who knows what is right these days. Are there really any absolutes?" We may or may not realize that we are drifting along on the stream of this world's ideas of living, obeying its unseen ruler, and following our own impulses and imaginations much as we did before we turned to Christ.[5]

It is not necessary to live like this. God has provided a way out. He has given us everything we need for lives pleasing to Him and to ourselves, and helpful to others. We must take time to discover God's will, and we must choose to do it. What counts is action, not wishes. As J. Oswald Sanders has expressed it, "We are as close to God as we *choose* to be, not as we *want* to be."

A. W. Tozer emphasized the critical need for adequate time alone with God:

> We Christians must simplify our lives or lose untold treasures on earth and in eternity. Modern civilization is so complex as to make the devotional life all but impossible.
>
> Science, which has provided men with certain material comforts, has robbed them of their souls by surrounding them with a world hostile to their existence. . . .
>
> One way the civilized world destroys men is by preventing them from thinking their own thoughts.
>
> Our "vastly improved methods of communication" of which the short-sighted boast so loudly now enable a few men in strategic centers to feed into millions of minds alien thought–stuff, ready-made and pre-digested. A little effortless assimilation of these borrowed ideas and the average man has done all the thinking he will or can do. This subtle brainwashing goes on day after day. . . .
>
> The need for solitude and quietness was never greater than it is today.[6]

Personal Application

1. What ideas in this chapter could help me improve my quiet time?

2. Which of these should I begin to do right away?

NOTES   1. *Quiet Time* (InterVarsity Press, 1945).
2. A. W. Tozer, *That Incredible Christian* (Christian Publications, Inc., 1964).
3. Daniel 6:10, NIV.
4. Isaiah 50:4, NIV.
5. Ephesians 2:2-3, PH.
6. A. W. Tozer, *The Best of A. W. Tozer*, compiled by Warren W. Wiersbe (Baker Book House, 1978), pages 149–151.

11

Improving Your Quiet Time

O Satisfy us in the morning with
Thy lovingkindness, that we
may sing for joy and be glad all
our days.
(Psalm 90:14)

To enjoy a vital and profitable quiet time, we must cultivate sensitivity to the Holy Spirit's leading, coupled with a spirit of order and method. The quiet time needs both flexibility and structure, both freedom and form. To insist on total freedom and refuse to plan ahead may indicate laziness in disguise and rob us of maximum profit. Planning can prevent aimlessness and monotony. It can help us reach our goal of knowing the Lord and His will better.

Yet as we seek to cultivate good habits in our quiet time, we must beware of being so method-centered that we meet a *plan* rather than a Person. Aim primarily at meeting with God. The great thing in your time with Him is not how much you get done. The great thing is having fellowship with Him. And good habits contribute to that fellowship.

Choose a Place
For many people it is best to have a *regular place* for meeting God. A familiar place keeps our thoughts from being diverted by

73

new surroundings. The place you choose should have few distractions and interruptions. It should be as private as possible.

Jesus said, "When you pray, go away by yourself, all alone, and shut the door behind you and pray to your Father secretly."[1] Jesus Himself frequently made the effort to get alone in quiet places. Sometimes, however, this is not possible. Jonathan Goforth, a missionary to China who lived with his family in a crowded house, obtained the privacy he needed by standing in a corner facing the wall as he read and prayed. The Lord's presence can turn any surroundings into a holy place of fellowship and power.

It is best, however, not to have your quiet time in bed. Get up, wash your face, do whatever you find necessary to be wide awake. If you shave or dress before your time with God, guard against letting slowness or distractions nibble away your time. And beware of reading the morning newspaper first and letting it rob you of adequate time with the Lord.

Find a *bodily position* that will keep you alert. This varies from person to person and from time to time. Some people like to sit, as David did at times, or to stand in prayer, a position common in both Testaments. Others find that walking in prayer— either outdoors or back and forth indoors—helps them concentrate and stay awake. Kneeling before the Lord may help us bend our will to God. Lying face down on the floor may help us humble ourselves before Him and feel our desperate need of Him.

C. S. Lewis, in *Letters to Malcolm, Chiefly on Prayer*, writes, "Kneeling does matter, but other things matter even more. A concentrated mind and a sitting body make for a better prayer than a kneeling body and a mind half asleep."[2]

Prepare Your Heart

Before you utter a request, rest your heart on the thought that you are in the presence of a living Person and that your goal is spiritual contact with Him. Thank the Lord that He loves you, desires your fellowship, and promises to reward you as you seek Him. Worship Him, thanking Him for His greatness, holiness, love, power, beauty, and perfection. Whether or not our worship brings us immediate satisfaction, it pleases our wonderful Father who seeks people to worship Him. Thanksgiving and praise honor

Him and draw us from being too occupied with ourselves and our earthly concerns.

Pause and humble yourself before God. Do not hastily rush into your requests. *Acknowledge your dependence on Him and affirm your dedication,* presenting yourself reverently before Him: "Father, You are my God and I am your servant. I am here to learn from you, to pray according to Your will, and to do what You say. Please help me."

Learn to Concentrate

Write down major truths that you learn. This sharpens your thoughts and helps you remember them. A notebook that you use just for your quiet time helps you to meditate and to share with others as you have an opportunity to do so. It is also a blessing to review your earlier thoughts. But be careful not to spend too much time writing.

Take control of your wandering thoughts. As often as your mind goes off on a tangent, bring it back with quiet firmness and without scolding yourself. Often you can pray about whatever distracted you, then resume where you left off. When things come to mind that need to be done, write them down and pray about them. If you merely try to push them out of your mind, they will continue to nag at you. Also try praying aloud or in a whisper. This can help you stay alert, especially if you are sleepy.

Ask God to increase your ability to concentrate both in prayer and at other times. Brother Lawrence wrote, "One way to recollect the mind easily in the time of prayer, and preserve it in more tranquility, is not to let it wander too far at other times,"

Use a Prayer List

One help I often use for intercession during my quiet time is a prayer list with names of people for whom I want to pray. This keeps me from aimless mental wandering and from forgetting prayer opportunities and responsibilities. From time to time I revise the list, adding new names and needs and deleting others. Some people collect photos or cut pictures from prayer letters to use as reminders for prayer.

To add interest and broaden your praying, include one or

more people from the following categories, praying for both their spiritual progress and their personal needs:

- Family members and friends
- Your pastor and church
- Other Christians and Christian workers
- Missionaries
- Government leaders

Do not become a slave to any method. If your prayer list becomes a chore, rewrite it or pray without a list for awhile. If it becomes too long, divide it into two or three lists, using one each day. A prayer list should be a helpful servant, not a restricting master.

Include Several Types of Prayer

In your quiet time and other prayer times, include the various types of prayer listed below, though not necessarily in the order given. This will enrich your prayer times, making them more satisfying both to God and to yourself.

—*Worship God.* Praise Him for who He is.

—*Humble yourself.* Acknowledge your dependence on God and renew your dedication. Confess any unconfessed sins He brings to mind.

—*Pray for yourself.* Ask God to change you, as well as to bless you, and to give you what you need.

—*Pray for others.* Intercede for their salvation or spiritual growth and their special needs. Pray for God's work nearby and worldwide.

—*Give thanks.* Include thanksgiving for past and future blessings.

Vary Your Quiet Time

It is rewarding to occasionally have a quiet time that is wholly praise. Read through a Psalm, such as Psalm 103 or 145, pausing frequently to praise God for who He is and what He does. If you have time, thank God for the various people you usually pray for, and praise Him for what He has already done in their lives.

Or, after your regular time in the Word, review the events of the previous day, praising the Lord for His faithfulness in various situations. Go over the details of the coming day, praising Him in advance for His promised sufficiency and blessings.

If your quiet time becomes lifeless or tiresome, talk this over with the Lord. Also ask a friend to pray with you that time after time your soul may know the refreshment that comes from the presence of the Lord.[3]

Review your quiet time plan occasionally, changing any part that needs it. Variety can help keep your time fresh. (Appendix A gives further help when you feel you need a change.)

Develop an Expectant Attitude

The following excerpt from *Quiet Time* describes a basic attitude essential for vital fellowship with God:

> In all our reading of His Word and in all our praying, our greatest need is a warm and living and expectant faith, what Charles Finney called an "affectionate confidence" in God . . . The one object of our devotions should be to eliminate everything that will keep us from believing God utterly.[4]

We are to come to our quiet time in faith, expecting God to meet us and teach us. As we pray, we are to expect Him to hear and answer. As we leave for our daily activities, we are to expect His loving presence to be with us, giving us guidance and power. This expectancy may at times be a simple choice to believe, or it may include an assured feeling of confidence. Either way, God promises to work as we trust Him. Bring to God again and again your desire to cultivate good habits of prayer and feeding on His Word. Pray that in new ways you will experience God and give Him pleasure in your daily meetings with Him.

Personal Application

1. Which suggestion in this chapter should I begin to use now?
2. What else do I eventually want to change in my quiet time?

NOTES   1. Matthew 6:6, *The Living Bible.*
       2. C. S. Lewis, *Letters to Malcolm, Chiefly on Prayer* (Harcourt Brace Jovanovitch, 1963), page 18.
       3. Acts 3:19, PH.
       4. *Quiet Time* (InterVarsity Press, 1945), page 4.

12

Mining Riches
from God's Word

How blessed is the man . . .
[whose] delight is in
the law of the Lord,
And in His Law he meditates
day and night.
And he will be like a tree firmly
planted by streams of water,
Which yields its fruit
in its season,
And its leaf does not wither;
And in whatever he does, he
prospers.
(Psalm 1:1-3)

Several translations begin Psalm 1 with, "Oh the joys." Oh the multiplied pleasures, the contentment, and the well-being of the person who delights in God's Word! He spends time reflecting on it. As a result, his life displays spiritual health and fruit, and everything he does is successful—his studies, his work, his relationships, and his Christian service.

Meditate and Pray

Psalm 1 does not *command* us to meditate; it merely describes the benefits. God's word in Joshua 1:8 is stronger: "You shall meditate on it day and night." Again the Lord spells out the secret of success—always having the Word of God in our mouth, feeding on it day and night, sharing it with others, and obeying it.

Ruminate is a synonym for *meditate*. A cow ruminates several times a day; after swallowing her food, she brings it back and chews the cud over and over. God wants us to "ruminate" on His Word in order to fully know and obey Him. "Chew" it prayerfully, taking time to reflect on its truths and their application.

Meditating on God's Word profits little without the Holy Spirit's enlightenment. Our minds can grasp the facts we read, but only God's Spirit gives insight into their meaning and application. He enables us to digest truth and make it part of our lives, and often He gives His enlightenment in answer to prayer. Make David's request your own as you meditate on God's Word: "Give me understanding, and I will keep Your law and obey it with all my heart."[1]

Available Treasures

Imagine that one afternoon a good friend who owns a diamond mine invites you for a tour. As you walk through the mine, you see glass-like objects here and there.

"Are those diamonds?"

"Yes. They are diamonds in the rough, before we clean and cut them."

"I've never seen a rough diamond before!"

"You may have one if you like."

"Really?"

"In fact, you can have all the diamonds you can find and carry out in five minutes."

How would you react? If you were a man, your pockets would bulge and you would have trouble walking. If you were a woman, it would take both hands to carry your purse. What an offer! You would be rich for life.

In His Word the Lord of the universe offers us priceless gems to make us rich beyond our wildest imaginings—rich in heart, rich in mind, rich in service, rich in knowing Him. The spiritual riches are there for the taking, and there is no limit to what we can have. Countless treasures await us as we seek to know Him better: "Oh, the depth of the riches both of the wisdom and knowledge of God!"[2]

Read Consecutively

Henrietta Mears, a well-known Bible teacher, wrote:

Who should read the Bible?
The young to know how to live;

The old to know how to die;
The ignorant for wisdom;
The learned for humility;
The rich for warning;
The poor for enrichment.
It is a Book for all sorts and kinds of people.[3]

If you are new to Bible reading, read through the New Testament before spending much time in the Old Testament, except for Psalms and Proverbs. You will better understand the Old Testament after you have read the entire New Testament two or three times.

If you want to begin with a Gospel, Luke and John are rich. If starting with a shorter book appeals to you, try Philippians or 1 Thessalonians. Your goal is to establish the delightful habit of reading some of the New Testament daily, and to read it through two or three times as soon as possible.

The first few mornings after I lead a person to Christ, I meet him for a quiet time and help him begin a reading program. I like to start him in the short, joyful book of Philippians. It is full of practical treasures, and completing a book in a few days gives a feeling of achievement: "The desire accomplished is sweet to the soul."[4] I often encourage a person to read Philippians two or even three times before doing the same with Colossians, mining rich nuggets with each reading. Next I recommend 1 Thessalonians with its forceful truths about godly living and Christ's return.

Reading one chapter a day is a good pace. However, the Holy Spirit at times leads a person to read only a few verses, and at other times to complete two or three chapters. Reading each book several times helps to impress its teachings on our minds.

After Philippians, Colossians and 1 Thessalonians, I suggest reading the Gospel of John. It exalts the Lord Jesus Christ, showing Him as the divine Son of God through His claims, miracles, and teachings. Although John is a good place to start a person in a quiet time, I prefer the three shorter books. However, no matter where one starts, a wealth of spiritual truths awaits discovery.

After a person reads John, I encourage him to continue on through the rest of the New Testament, reading each book at least twice. When he completes Revelation, he can go to Matthew and proceed through the entire New Testament. Many people enjoy reading a shorter book after each Gospel, for a change of pace.

Diligence and Understanding

Some of God's treasures are easy to discover. We must dig to find others. Then we must meditate to cut and polish each diamond of truth so that its distinctive beauties shine forth. We must obey its teachings to make them part of our lives and display His beauty.[5] How many of God's spiritual treasures have you made your own? Are you diligent to accumulate new riches daily, enough for yourself and others, or are you frequently in want?

Diligence requires taking sufficient time each day for meditation on the rich truths God brings to our attention. E. M. Bounds wrote that "God's acquaintance is not made by pop calls. God does not bestow His gifts on the casual or hasty comers and goers. Much [time] alone with God is the secret of knowing Him and of influence with Him."[6]

The following questions can help you meditate, both in your quiet time and during the day. They are based on the four ways the Scriptures can profit us: "All Scripture is inspired by God and profitable for teaching, for reproof, for correction, for training in righteousness; that the man of God may be adequate, equipped for every good work."[7] To become more adequate and equipped, ask these four questions as you meditate on God's Word:

- *What should I know?*   *(teaching)*
  - *What should I forsake?*   *(reproof)*
  - *How should I change?*   *(correction)*
- *How should I live?*   *(training in righteousness)*

The first and fourth questions are the basic ones.

Answers to the question *What should I know?* should mold our thinking, while answers to the question *How should I live?* should mold our character and actions. These two questions are closely related, for our lives are shaped by what we think.[8]

Before we can live properly, we must be clear from God's

Word about what He desires. Each of the two middle questions has a two-way focus—on changes in our thinking and changes in our lives—what to forsake and change in our thinking, and what to forsake and change in our living.

Try using these four questions as you meditate on your favorite verses. As J. S. James wrote:

> God speaks to us through His Word. There are countless other books, helpful and inspiring, written by godly men. Put these books on the second shelf. Put God's Book on a shelf by itself. If you have plenty of time for both, good; but give His Book first place.

Personal Application

1. What thought or suggestion in this chapter can most help me feed on God's Word more profitably?
2. What do I plan to do about this?

NOTES
1. Psalm 119:34, NIV.
2. Romans 11:33.
3. Henrietta Mears, *431 Quotes from the Notes of Henrietta C. Mears* (Regal Books, 1970), page 63.
4. Proverbs 13:19, KJV.
5. 1 Peter 2:9.
6. E. M. Bounds, *Power Through Prayer* (Baker Book House, 1963), page 44.
7. 2 Timothy 3:16–17.
8. Proverbs 4:23, GNB.

13

Our Emotions
and God's Word

> Everyone then who hears these
> words of mine and puts them
> into practice is like a sensible
> man who builds his house on the
> rock. Down came the rain and
> up came the floods, while the
> winds blew and roared upon
> that house—and it did not fall
> because its foundations were on
> the rock.
> (Matthew 7:24–25, PH)

Prayer brings incredible results. It is God's way of linking His boundless power with our human weakness to accomplish His will in the world. He invites us to be involved with Him, tell Him our needs, and see Him do remarkable things, often beyond what we have asked or thought.

Yet some people try prayer and end up disillusioned. They abandon their prayer boat on the shoals of disappointment when their wishes are not granted, or they let it bob idly at its moorings through laziness or unbelief. They give up instead of sailing steadily on by faith, failing to follow more closely God's instructions on how to pray effectively.

God's Word forms a solid foundation for all that we do. David exemplifies the view of the Scriptures that fosters a vital, God-pleasing prayer life:

The words of the Lord are flawless.

All Thy commandments are truth.

Every one of Thy righteous ordinances is everlasting.

Therefore I esteem right all Thy precepts concerning everything.[1]

With such an attitude, the Word can have a controlling influence in our praying, enabling God to impart motivation, wisdom, and even restraint as we pray.

God's Word Stimulates Prayer

Repeatedly the Bible exhorts us to pray:

> Watch and pray.
> Ask, and you will receive.
> Jesus told . . . them that they should always pray and not give up.
> Keep asking . . . keep seeking . . . keep knocking.
> Pray without ceasing.
> Call to Me, and I will answer you.[2]

God's commands provide our greatest motivation for continuing in prayer. They liberate us from being bound by our feelings. They offer us the most amazing freedom a person can have—the freedom of speaking with God as our own Father and personal friend.

In *Prayer and Modern Man* Jacques Ellul points out that prayer is not a binding requirement but a liberating opportunity. Viewing God's command to pray as an impersonal "law" with a threat of penalty can make prayer an irksome duty. Instead, His command to pray is personal, addressed to each of us by One who loves us. Picture yourself opening an important looking invitation that reads, "The King invites you to spend time with Him and to present your requests." Who would say no to that?

David not only considered God's commands dependable, he also delighted in them. He prayed,

> I will walk at liberty,
> For I seek thy precepts.
> I shall delight in Thy commandments,
> Which I love.
> And I shall lift up my hands to Thy commandments, which I love;
> And I will meditate on Thy statutes.
> Thy testimonies also are my delight;
> They are my counselors.[3]

God's commands deserve our love as much as His promises. Each commandment is a promissory note, assuring us God's blessings if we obey. This is strikingly true of His commandments to pray. They usher us into the presence of our generous Father-King and give us the key to His treasure house. As we choose to obey His commands, His Spirit motivates and empowers us.

Depend on the Word, Not Feelings

My son once said, "Dad, at times my prayers just seem to bounce off the ceiling." I assured him I sometimes felt the same way. But our feelings are not the key to the Lord's hearing or answering. None of the conditions for answered prayer involve how we feel. ⎯

A liberating principle in prayer and in our daily lives is to *depend on the Word, not feelings.*

Sometimes we let our feelings determine whether or not we pray. "I am just not in a praying mood today," we think. "I can't pray when I feel like this." But how we feel should not be the basis on which we decide whether or not to pray. Charles H. Spurgeon wrote,

> We should pray when we are in a praying mood, for it would be ✔
> sinful to neglect so fair an opportunity. We should pray when we
> are not in a praying mood because it would be dangerous to
> remain in so unhealthy a condition.

Though we know better, how natural it is to think God's answers are linked to our feelings. When we feel liberated and bold as we come to the throne of grace, we imagine that our requests are rated "Urgent" and will bring immediate results. When we feel discouraged or unspiritual, we mutter a few feeble prayers, doubting that God will hear them. On some unconscious level, we believe that our emotional state affects how God evaluates and answers our prayers.

Feelings are not out of place. Many people in the Bible—including Jeremiah, Hannah, the Psalmists, Jesus Christ, and Paul—prayed with deep feeling and urgent pleading. If God gives an intense concern, we can implore Him vigorously. If we have a special consciousness of God's presence or of the Holy Spirit's liberation, we should enjoy it. But if not, we can still pray.

This lesson on prayer has especially helped me. Though I sometimes pray or offer praise with a delightful awareness that the Spirit is leading me along, at other times I don't *feel* such liberty. Either way, if I am praying according to God's conditions, I can be confident that the Lord is hearing.

Though the Holy Spirit often gives joyous feelings or compelling burdens, praying "in the Spirit"[4] does not refer to how we feel as we pray. It means praying in dependence on the Holy Spirit and being directed and helped by Him as we pray. It means praying according to the will of the Holy Spirit as it is recorded in God's Word.

Christians have varying emotional responses in prayer. Some often have intense emotions as they pray. Others have experiences that are on a more subdued or intellectual level. No one pattern of experience is best. Each of us should pray in his or her own way, without coveting or trying to duplicate the emotions or responses of another. In our basic emotional responses, as in our personalities, God made each of us unique so that we may enjoy Him and enjoy prayer in our own way. He wants fellowship with our particular personality and will give us the emotions that He thinks are best for us.

Richard Halverson, the Chaplain of the United States Senate, explains the relationship between faith and feelings:

> Authentic faith depends upon the Word of God no matter how strong one's feeling may be to the contrary. The Bible is to the believer what the instrument panel is to the pilot. The basic discipline is to learn to *believe against feelings*. Feelings are a result of believing . . . not a basis for believing.[5]

Satan constantly tries to make us trust our feelings or to focus our attention on experiences or how things *seem* rather than to depend on God's Word. He tempts us to existential, experience-based living that considers inner feelings more dependable than the Scriptures. He knows that this will keep us from living a steady, maturing Christian life. Yielding to this temptation hinders progress and leads to instability.

Any of us can become sidetracked into feeling-centered living. We can think that to be honest or genuine we must respond to our emotional impulses and preferences; that unless we act as we feel, we are insincere, not expressing our true selves. *But feelings are not the only authentic part of our inner person. We also have a mind and a will.* We can turn our minds to God's commands and with our will choose to obey, even when our feelings depress or distract us. We can choose to be governed by God and His Word rather than by our subjective inner state.

> Asked late in life if he always prayed with a consciousness of joy, Hudson Taylor explained that generally his heart felt like wood when praying. But this didn't prevent results, for Taylor reported that most of his major victories came through "emotionless prayer."[6]

Disturbing Emotions

Emotions are a wonderful part of life. When stabilized by God, they motivate and nourish us. Yet how often feelings of discouragement, confusion, and spiritual emptiness retard our spiritual progress. Such feelings can come from natural causes. Are you getting enough sleep? Do you schedule an occasional change of pace to avoid excessive pressure? Do you need a medical checkup, better nutrition, or more regular meals? Do you need to say no to activities that are not the best use of your gifts and time? Sometimes such practical steps can restore freshness to one's prayer life.

Fluctuating emotions are a normal part of being human. Our physical lives move in cycles with peaks of vitality and troughs of diminished energy. This influences our feelings about God and life. Even godly King David found that his sense of God's presence varied, and the apostle Paul recorded some of his emotional ups and downs.

Distressing emotions can also come from unconfessed sin. We cannot enter God's presence while disregarding sin in our lives and expect to enjoy Him as we normally do. At times we know the specific sin that is disrupting our fellowship with God. At other times, when we feel *vaguely* guilty, we are not to rummage and scratch around until we find some sin to confess. Instead we can simply ask God to show us any sin that is hindering our fellowship with Him. He is more interested in revealing it to us than we are in discovering it. If He does not show us anything definite to confess, we can thank Him for our righteousness in Christ and proceed with confidence, whether or not our feelings coincide.

The Holy Spirit is not the author of those clouds of *undefined* guilt feelings. He is the encourager, not the accuser. As we continue in His Word, He reveals sin specifically, either immediately when we ask, or later. Then we can confess and be cleansed. And for those sins He has not revealed specifically, we can pray, "Who can discern his errors? Acquit me of hidden faults."[7]

When our times of prayer lack emotional freshness, we might pray as Samuel McComb did:

> Gracious Father, quicken the heart of Your servant. Refresh, I beseech You, the dullness and dryness of his inner life. Grant him perseverance that he may never abandon the effort to pray, even though it brings for a time no comfort or joy. Teach him to pray the prayer that relieves his burdened spirit and brings Your blessing.[8]

Encouraging Emotions

The Holy Spirit often uses the Word to lift my heart and transform my feelings. Often the verses that most powerfully lift me out of spiritual dryness or discouragement are ones that turn my thoughts to God Himself. During the past year Romans 11:22 has restored to my heart a warm appreciation of God's undeserved love and kindness toward me: "Behold then the kindness . . . of God." This verse has often led me to think about Psalm 31:19: "How great is Thy goodness, which Thou hast stored up for those who fear Thee, which Thou hast wrought for those who take refuge in Thee, before the sons of men!" I often reflect on the song, "God is so good. God is so good. He's so good to me."

Reviewing God's specific blessings also encourages me. I often read Psalm 16:6, which teaches that the boundary lines of my life have fallen in pleasant places. My life has included struggles, failures, disappointments, and testings, but also the presence and blessing of God Himself. I paraphrase this verse as a prayer to the Lord: "You have certainly made my life pleasant and my situations delightful," and I thank Him for the specific ways He has done this. Psalm 23:6 gives me the same confidence for the future, as I thank the Lord that "Surely goodness and Your abundant love and kindness will follow me every day of *this* life, and throughout eternity I will live with You in the place You are preparing for me." These truths lift my emotions and stimulate praise.

When I feel fearful or inadequate, the Spirit often uses Zechariah 4:6 to restore my confidence. I remind God, "Lord, I don't have to be adequate, because it's not by might nor by power but by Your Spirit that my work will be done well." Praying over 1 Corinthians 15:10 also removes the uncertainties of many situations: "By your grace Lord, I have been what I have been, in spite of myself, and by Your grace I will be what I will be in the future. Thank You that the secret is Your grace plus hard work, not abilities that I lack."

Through my daily reading or through special verses, God often restores confidence and joy to my heart. Romans 15:13 says, "Now may the God of hope fill you with all joy and peace in believing, that you may abound in hope by the power of the Holy Spirit." In verse four of the same chapter, we read that through the encouragement of the Scriptures we have hope. The Spirit and the Word work together to give God's encouragement in place of depressing emotions. Andrew Murray writes in *The Prayer Life,*

> Oh, that we but understood that the Holy Spirit is essentially the Spirit of the Word and the Spirit of prayer! He will cause the Word to become a joy and a light in our souls, and He will also most surely help us in prayer to know the mind and will of God, and find in it our delight.[9]

Even when the Lord does not revive my emotions, I can pray (or witness or read the Word) with confidence if I am walking in the light He has given.

Simplicity or Eloquence?

Just as feelings have nothing to do with prayer's effectiveness, neither does eloquence. It is easy to think that a beautiful prayer with correct grammar and a bit of flourish speeds into God's presence and receives His immediate attention, but a stumbling and muddled prayer is ignored. Perhaps William Gurnall has described your experience concerning prayer:

> Sometimes you hear another pray with much freedom and fluency, while you can hardly get out a few broken words. Hence you are ready to accuse yourself and admire him as if the gilding of the key makes it open the door better.

Our oratory, our persuasive logic, our orderliness, our theological precision—none of these unlocks the door to God's presence. Such things may enhance public prayer, but they have no influence on God. Though God often uses a Spirit-filled, eloquent prayer to edify, encourage, and arouse His people, a simple prayer equally delights God and brings answers.

Recently a woman said to me, "A few months ago I heard you say that eloquence in prayer was not necessary. That helped me. Then God taught me that neither is originality important. I used to feel that if I could pray in enough different ways, God would be impressed."

We somehow consider variety more powerful than dull repetition, so we pray for a person to be saved, forgiven, born again, made a new creature, given eternal life, or that he will open the door of his heart, receive Christ, turn to the Lord, or believe in Christ. Surely, we think, such prayer influences God more than merely asking daily, "Lord save him." But if God answers any one of these requests, He answers them all. Whatever words we use, God understands.

Yet I sometimes experience a burden, an impassioned groaning, so that I just cannot move on in prayer to the next person or request. In such prayer, the Holy Spirit may lead me to plead repeatedly for a certain thing, perhaps in different ways. But this is not the same as thinking that if I can just voice my request in enough ways or with enough feeling, the Lord will be more inclined to hear and answer. Originality may motivate me, but it does not impress God.

The same is true of loudness or intensity. Sometimes I pray enthusiastically and forcefully, increasing the volume until my wife reminds me, "Dear, God isn't deaf!" There is nothing wrong with praying this way, but God just as easily hears an unemotional whisper. Being right with God is the important thing. "The effective prayer of a righteous man can accomplish much."[10]

Nor do we assure answers by stretching out requests, as though prolonged prayers and many words impress the Lord. One man commented, "I used to feel that if I prayed less than thirty minutes for a person, my prayer was almost useless." Lengthening our requests is not a condition for answers. Self-effort is not a key to successful prayer. It is "not by force of numbers nor by individual effort, but by My Spirit, says the Lord of hosts."[11]

It is not that long prayers are unacceptable to God. Taking time to explain details to the Lord can clarify our thoughts and help focus our praying. Often David, relating to God as his friend, explained his problems and reviewed his situation in great detail. Much time spent with God in prayer has a transforming effect on us and on our faith, but we are not heard just because of our heaped-up words.

False and True Emotions in Prayer

The prophet Isaiah in chapters fifty-eight and fifty-nine tells of people who experienced emotional satisfaction in their prayer life, but were guilty of serious sins that kept God from hearing and answering their prayers. God was displeased with them: "Yet they seek Me day by day, and delight to know My ways. . . . They ask Me for just decisions, they delight in the nearness of God."[12]

Though they felt close to God, their closeness was only imagined. From God's viewpoint they were not near, for their hearts were far from Him. Their attempted approach to Him included fasting, sackcloth, and ashes, all signifying self-denial and mourning. "Why have we fasted and Thou dost not see?" they asked, reproaching God. "Why have we humbled ourselves and Thou does not notice?"[13] Neither enjoyment nor misery made their prayers acceptable because they were not seeking Him with a desire to do His will.

The Lord leads some people to pray with a heavily burdened heart, with tears, groanings, urgent pleas, and great agonizings. Such prayer is acceptable as long as one relies on God in simple faith, not trying to earn an answer by emotional distress or fervor. We should not fear or avoid emotions, since both sorrow and joy have a beneficial, healing effect on us and can be a true part of Spirit-led praying. We should feel free to pray emotionally, but we should not consider it the only effective way to pray. Feelings can be deceiving and are not a reliable gauge of how pleased God is with our prayers or our lives.

A. W. Tozer, in *Man: the Dwelling Place of God*, writes,

> The heart of a man is like a musical instrument and may be played upon by the Holy Spirit, by an evil spirit or by the spirit of man himself. Religious emotions are very much the same, no matter who the player may be. Many enjoyable feelings may be aroused within the soul by low or even idolatrous worship.[14]

Tozer goes on to describe a nominally Christian woman kneeling before a religious statue, "breathless with adoration," feeling love, awe, and reverence as surely as if she were worshipping God, who has expressly forbidden bowing or praying to any statue, picture, or idol.[15] Tozer also explains that we cannot brush aside as mere imaginings the ecstatic mystical experiences of people such as Hindus, spiritists, and occultists, who sometimes have genuine encounters with some spirit or power beyond themselves, but not with the true God.

In *The Death of a Guru*, Rabindranath R. Maharaj describes his intensely pleasurable religious flights as a Hindu prodigy. Later he tells of terrifying experiences after the spirits he was worshipping had gained control over him through the enticement of mystical delights. Sometimes Christians, searching for spiritual experiences or experimenting with eastern religious practices, such as transcendental meditation, are likewise led into spiritual ecstacies that do not come from God.

Lesser perils can also steal their way into our times of prayer. Centuries ago, Madame Guyon wrote, "I made many mistakes through allowing myself to be too much taken up with my interior joys."

My sister-in-law, who has a close and effective walk with the Lord, once said that sometimes after an exceptionally rapturous time alone with God, she would go through one of her worst days in her attitudes toward trials, household duties, and family members. She found her days were more under the Holy Spirit's control when she moderated her emotions during her quiet time, not letting them dominate. She still exulted in the Lord, but she reserved more time for the serious business of meditating on God's commandments and praying through the details of her day. Before closing her prayer time, she acknowledged her total dependence on God and renewed her dedication to do His will in the realities of family life. Then as she prepared meals and washed dishes, she was not relying on an exhilarating quiet time but on God Himself, indwelling and controlling her by His Spirit.

David practiced this kind of balance. He coupled his delight in God and the Scriptures with a careful consideration of his personal ways, in order to obey the Lord's commandments.[16] He had a healthy emphasis on emotions, balanced by thoughtful attention to obedience.

Oswald Chambers wrote that to be *enchanted* by Jesus Christ ✓ is one thing, but to be *changed* by Him is quite another thing. Enchantment has no significance if it does not make Christ our dominant interest and our only Master. Feelings of adoration are delightful, but letting Him captivate our mind and will in a growing obedience is far more important.

Learning His truth is sometimes routine, sometimes pleasurable, sometimes painful. As we choose to conform our thoughts to His Word and obey Him, He molds our emotions, both in prayer and in our daily lives.

If we live cleansed, abiding lives, and if we pray in Jesus' name, according to God's will, with faith, God will hear us. Our feelings, the length of our prayers, or their eloquence are not the basis for confident praying. We must rely upon God and His Word.

Personal Application

1. Are there any ways in which I have been letting my emotions hinder my effectiveness in prayer?
2. What can I do to prevent this in the future?

NOTES 1. Based on Psalm 12:6, NIV; and 119:151, 160, and 128.
2. Matthew 26:41, KJV; John 16:24; Luke 18:1, NIV; Luke 11:9, NASB

margin notes; 1 Thessalonians 5:17; Jeremiah 33:3.

3. Psalm 119:45, 47–48, 24.
4. Ephesians 6:18.
5. Richard C. Halverson, *Somehow Inside of Eternity* (New York International Bible Society, 1978), page 46.
6. Dick Eastman, *Change the World School of Prayer* (World Literature Crusade, n.d.), page D-120.
7. Psalm 19:12.
8. Samuel McComb, *A Book of Prayer* (Dodd, Mead and Company, 1912).
9. Andrew Murray, *The Prayer Life* (Moody Press, n.d.), page 89.
10. James 5:16.
11. Zechariah 4:6, using the literal meaning of the Hebrew words *might* and *power.*
12. Isaiah 58:2.
13. Isaiah 58:3.
14. A. W. Tozer, *Man: The Dwelling Place of God* (Christian Publications, Inc., 1966), page 122.
15. Exodus 20:4–5.
16. Psalm 119:59–60.

Devotion and Commitment

> Resolved: that all men
> should live for the glory of God.
> Resolved second: that whether
> others do or not, I will.
> —Jonathan Edwards

God is looking for men and women with committed hearts, men and women who earnestly desire to know Christ intimately and who follow Him diligently. Such people open themselves to God's teaching and empowering, and God will reward them with a liberty and effectiveness in life and in prayer that others seldom imagine. In 2 Chronicles 16:9 (*The Living Bible*) we read,

> For the eyes of the Lord search back and forth across the whole earth, looking for people whose hearts are perfect toward him, so that he can show his great power in helping them.

Christ Desires Our Fellowship

The Lord of heaven and earth yearns to see our face and hear our voice. He feels about us as the bridegroom in Song of Solomon felt about his bride: "Your voice is sweet, and your face is lovely."[1] Our daily quiet time is important to Him.

In Dr. Robert Munger's motivating booklet, *My Heart Christ's Home*, a young Christian tells how he yielded the various rooms of his heart to Christ and learned that He desired his fellowship.

We walked next into the drawing room. I liked this room. It was intimate and pleasant, with a fireplace, comfortable chairs, a bookcase and a quiet atmosphere. The Lord seemed pleased with it.

"This is indeed a delightful room," He said, "Let us come here often and we can have fellowship together." As a young Christian I could think of nothing I would rather do than have a few minutes apart with Christ in intimate comradeship. He promised, "I will be here every morning early. Meet me and we will start the day together."

So morning after morning, I came downstairs to the drawing room. He would take the Bible from the bookcase, open it, and we would read together. He warmed my heart as He unfolded to me its truths, and revealed His love and grace toward me. Those were wonderful hours together.

But little by little, under the presure of many responsibilities, our quiet times together shortened. This was not at all intentional, I was just too busy. Finally I began now and then to miss a day, then several days, to study for examinations at the university or for other urgent activities.

One morning as I rushed down the steps eager to be on my way, I glanced into the drawing room and saw the Lord sitting there alone. I thought in dismay, 'He is my guest. I invited Him into my heart as Lord of my home. And yet here I am neglecting Him.' With downcast glance I went in and said, "Blessed Master, have you been here all these mornings?" "Yes," He said, "I told you I would be here every morning to meet with you." Even more ashamed, I asked His forgiveness, which He readily granted. He said, "The trouble with you is this. You have been thinking of the quiet time as a factor in your own spiritual progress but have forgotten that this hour means something to Me also. Remember, I love you. I have redeemed you at a great cost. I desire your fellowship. Do not neglect this hour, if only for My sake. Whatever else may be your desire, remember I want your fellowship."

The truth that Christ wants my fellowship, that He loves me and waits for me, has done more to transform my quiet time than any other single fact. Don't let Christ wait alone in the drawing room of your heart.[2]

Unreserved Commitment

One day on the dusty road from Jerusalem to Damascus, a brilliant and prominent man named Saul met someone who revolutionized his life. As Saul approached Damascus, obsessed with a burning passion to destroy the followers of Christ, he suddenly saw a light brighter than an unclouded midday sun. Blinded, he fell to the ground and heard a voice, obviously the voice of God, calling his name.

"Saul, Saul, why are you persecuting Me?"

Saul cried out. "Who art Thou, Lord?"

Then came the shattering answer, "I am Jesus the Nazarene whom you are persecuting."[3]

In that moment Saul realized that *Jesus was God* and that in persecuting Christians, he had been persecuting God, for as members of Christ's body Christians were also part of God.

Many concerns could have flashed through Saul's mind: his family, all staunch Jews; his friends, strict religious Pharisees who shared Saul's hatred for Christ and His followers; his finances; his promising future as a Jewish leader. Were he to acknowledge Jesus as God, Paul the hunter would become the hunted. Though he was the son of an influential Jewish family and a Roman citizen by birth (others paid huge fees and bribes for that privilege), Saul would join the low-born, despised Christian community, followers of the politically and religiously hated Jesus of Nazareth.

In that brief moment outside Damascus Saul made his choice. His second question propelled him into a life and ministry that would change cities, countries, and civilizations, making him perhaps the greatest man who ever lived apart from Jesus Christ Himself.

Paul's second question was, "What shall I do, Lord?"[4]

This question, which acknowledged Christ as God and Lord, meant total surrender with no turning back. It was the indispensable first of many hard choices in Saul's life—his first big yes to Christ's lordship and control, to be followed by many daily yesses. From this time on, Saul became Paul, a new man, a history-changing man with a loyalty to Christ which few men or women have matched. Few have shown such unreserved surrender, such quickness to obey, such single-mindedness and joyful suffering, such unrelenting labor. Few have worked with such zeal or been as mightily used of God.

In Philippians 3, Paul summarizes his goal in life, while belittling the cost. Jesus Christ has become the total focus of his life and ministry, the one goal that embraces all others.

> But whatever was to my profit I now consider loss for the sake of Christ. What is more, I consider everything a loss compared to the surpassing greatness of knowing Christ Jesus my Lord, for whose sake I have lost all things. I consider them rubbish, that I may gain Christ. . . . *I want to know Christ* and the power of His resurrection and the fellowship of sharing in His sufferings, becoming like Him in His death. . . .
>
> *One thing I do:* Forgetting what is behind and straining toward what is ahead, I press on *toward the goal* to win the prize for which God has called me heavenward in Christ Jesus.[5]

Paul's determined purpose was to fully know and experience his risen Lord. Jesus Christ was now the focal point of his devotion, his message, his prayer for others, and his joy in suffering. Paul had a heart for Christ that set him apart from those with good-but-lesser goals.

One thing I do," Paul said. "I concentrate on this. I bring all my energies to bear on this one thing. I forget all that lies behind me and go straight for the goal." Not, "Many things occupy my attention," but, "One thing I do."

Paul had a single purpose, to know Christ and to make Him known, and he gave himself to it wholeheartedly. This burning desire molded all Paul did and all he prayed.

Such a dedication will also mold us and focus our prayers around the central figure in all of God's purposes, the Lord Jesus Christ. The world needs more men and women whose only focus is Christ.

Single-minded Devotion

One such man was David. He was David the sinner, but also "a man after My heart, who will do all My will."[6] What a commendation. This was God's evaluation of the king who would be the famed ancestor of His Son, Jesus Christ. One cannot read far in the Psalms without realizing David's unique passion to know God:

> One thing I have asked from the Lord, that I shall seek;
> That I may dwell in the house of the Lord all the days of my life,
> To behold the beauty of the Lord,
> And to meditate in His temple. . . .
> When Thou didst say, "Seek My face," my heart said to Thee,
> "Thy face, O Lord, I shall seek."[7]

The wealthy Count Zinzendorf of Germany forsook all and centered his life around the risen, reigning Christ. At the age of four he said, "Be Thou mine and I will be Thine;" at ten, "I have one passion. It is He and He alone."

This childhood dedication lasted a lifetime. No wonder God used him to launch the Moravian missionary outreach, a remarkable movement that sent missionaries to many parts of the world, including America, in the early 1700s. The Moravian church is noted for its one-hundred-year, round-the-clock prayer meeting for missions. One out of every ninety-two members went out as a missionary. The movement was used by God to transform thousands, including John Wesley of England who, like Zinzendorf, demonstrated singular devotion to Christ.

In my travels in Asia I meet young men and women with hearts like this. These people stand out. Their desire to know Christ, their depth and discipline in the Word, their prayer life, their zeal and effectiveness in proclaiming Christ make them different. They are far from perfect, but they have a rare warmth and winsomeness. And God is using them.

Today God is looking for more followers of Christ with single-minded devotion—men and women who will give themselves to live for God's glory, to pray for the lost and for laborers, and to have an impact on the world for Christ.

Through the years the following thoughts from InterVarsity's *Quiet Time* have challenged me.

> There is a passion for Christ which it has been given to a very few to possess, but which has set those who have it apart forever from their fellow men.[8]

The trouble with the rest of us is that . . . [although] we are hard at work for Him, the freighted hours rush by leaving us scarcely time to give a thought to the Lover of our souls who is longing for our friendship. . . .

Amidst the terrific onrush of the apostasy, amidst the swirl of pleasure which is engulfing the majority of those who call themselves Christians, God has His own. . . . They are men and women whose faith and zeal burn brighter as the world's darkness deepens. They are ready to die . . . for their Lord. They are valiant for the truth, and wield the sword lustily on His behalf. Nevertheless, few have that passion for Christ which Paul expressed in the words, "To me, to live is Christ."[9]

There is reward for the obedient disciples, there is power and authority for the faithful disciples, there is glory of achievement for the zealous disciples. . . . But there is the whisper of His love, there is the joy of His presence, and the shining of His face for those who love Him for Himself alone.[10]

Personal Application
1. What stood out to me most in this chapter?
2. What decision or action does God want me to take?

NOTES   1. Song of Songs (Song of Solomon) 2:14, NIV.
        2. Robert Boyd Munger, My Heart Christ's Home (InterVarsity Press, 1954).
        3. Acts 22:6-8.
        4. Acts 22:10.
        5. Philippians 3:7-10, 13-14, NIV.
        6. Acts 13:22.
        7. Psalm 27:4, 8.
        8. Quiet Time (InterVarsity Press, 1945), page 24.
        9. Quiet Time, pages 24–25.
        10. Quiet Time, page 30, italics added.

15

Make Time for Prayer

> The little estimate we put on
> prayer is evident from the little
> time we give to it.
> —E. M. Bounds,
> Power Through Prayer

Albert Einstein commented, "The perfection of means and confusion of goals is the hallmark of our time." Einstein might have added other hallmarks: deadlines, haste, busyness, and untold hours spent in leisure pursuits that we "owe ourselves" as compensation for life's stresses. Our goals are confused, and we seldom have enough time to do anything well, or to do at all the things that are truly important. We lack time for fellowship with God and a growing and effective prayer life. R. A. Torrey has highlighted what is true for many of us:

> How little time the average Christian spends in prayer! We are too
> busy to pray, and so we are too busy to have power. We have a
> great deal of activity, but we accomplish little. . . . The power of
> God is lacking in our lives and in our work. We have not because
> we ask not.[1]

Does the real problem lie in the amount of time we have?
Every person in the world has twenty-four hours a day. The rich
have no more, the poor no less. Many of these hours are at our

discretion, to use as we choose. Going to work is our choice, for we could stay home and starve. We take time to eat and sleep each day. We take time to study, serve the Lord, and watch television. We can decide, and often do, to omit some of these activities and add others. On weekends we take time for extra sleep, extra study, sports, or friends. What we do with our time is largely our choice. We take time for the things we most want to do and the things we think are most important.

Yet how often we say, "I don't have time for a regular quiet time. I don't have time to pray." How often do we stifle the Holy Spirit's inner prompting with the rationalization, "As soon as these pressures are over, I'll start spending time with God." Such thoughts reveal our values. Our real problem lies in our priorities more than in the time available to us. There is enough time in each day for everything that is in the will of God.

Choose to Make Time

The answer is not in *having* time to pray but in *making* time. I must decisively make time for prayer—daily, weekly, and monthly. I do not find this easy. I find it harder to make time for prayer than to depend on God's Word rather than my feelings. Yet it is essential if I want to please God and live a significant life. S. D. Gordon reminds us that God's great people are those who pray. They do not *have* the time, but must *take* the time from other things that are important and pressing.[2] Here lies both the core of our problem and its solution. We must plan time to pray, eliminating some other obligation or activity that is appealing, important, or even urgent.

We are faced with a choice of faith. If we truly believe that genuine satisfaction and lasting success come from God, we must pray. If we truly believe that mere sincerity or activity or organization does not produce spiritual results, but that enduring work for God is accomplished only through His Spirit, then we *must* make time for prayer.

Prayer is an act of dependence, and often of desperation, but *supremely it is an act of faith*. It declares that without God we can do nothing; that we believe His Word that teaches, "Unless the Lord builds the house, they labor in vain who build it."[3]

Prayer is a major evidence of true faith. If there were no God, prayer would be a waste of time, a supreme exercise in futility, a mere talking to the walls. But since there is a God, prayer is indispensable. "He who comes to God must believe that He is, and that He is a rewarder of those who seek Him.[4] By prayer we affirm our confidence that He exists, listens, and answers. This affirmation pleases God. It strengthens our faith and enables us to know and reflect Him more. Prayer is worth the time we invest in it.

Jesus Christ faced pressures greater than ours: the whole city gathering at His door for healing; crowds running to meet His boat; more than 5000 people pressing around Him for a whole day of teaching. What golden opportunities to proclaim the Gospel and glorify the Father by His works.

Yet the Lord often left the eager crowds, not primarily to rest or plan or organize, but to _pray_. At times this meant a night without sleep.

Few of us would abandon a flourishing revival where we were the main speaker to get a few days alone in prayer. But Christ knew His priorities. He who had all power in heaven and earth considered adequate times of prayer as essential as His public service. So He _often_ withdrew and prayed. And He is our example.

> But the news about Him was spreading even farther, and great multitudes were gathering to hear Him and to be healed of their sicknesses. But He Himself would often slip away to the wilderness and pray. . . . He went off to the mountain to pray, and He spent the whole night in prayer to God.[5]

When a family member becomes critically ill, we suddenly find time to pray. When we are coping with disappointment or loss or failure, we find time to pray. When we are in desperate need of money, we pray. But how can we find time to pray in our ordinary schedules? Only through a firm conviction that prayer is indispensable if we are to please God, enjoy His blessings, and advance His Kingdom. We need a settled persuasion that it is not our efforts, not our gifts, but prayer that releases God's power in our lives and in the lives of others.

Regular Time

Making time for prayer generally begins with scheduling a daily appointment with God before the activities of the day crowd Him out or make us too tired to enjoy His fellowship. Keeping such an appointment with the Lord depends on a determined decision that we *will* get time with Him. To give priority to prayer, we must put such times ahead of even service, fellowship, and meetings. This demands discipline. Fifteen or twenty minutes a day can generally be worked into a busy schedule. As our friendship with the Lord deepens, we can increase the time.

When I was a young Christian, I decided to spend no less than twenty minutes a day listening to the Lord and talking with Him. As I matured, I found twenty minutes too short, so I increased it. Then through a challenge I heard, God prompted me to give Him one hour each day, half in His Word and half in prayer. It has been a life-changing habit from which I profit more and more.

God is looking for people who, in the swirl of short days and short nights, proclaim by their actions, "You are the most important person in my life. I dare not and will not neglect You, regardless of the urgency of other things." This is faith that honors God, and He honors those who honor Him.

The greater our spiritual responsibilities, the more time we need with God to seek His guidance, His empowering, and His protection. Prayer takes time, but it also saves time by multiplying our effectiveness. The dividends far surpass the investment.

Recently a Navigator staff person from Canada told me that his ministry team had found it difficult to win friends and converts at a university of 18,000 students. So for several months he and a team member met twice a month for a day of fasting and prayer. I asked about the outcome.

"A month ago," he said, "we showed a movie that presented Christ. To our surprise 2,000 students showed up. That's a big crowd for our university."

"What happened?"

"Lots happened. One hundred twenty people signed cards indicating they were committing themselves to Christ, and 260 others asked for further information!"

I was impressed. "Although you haven't been able to contact all of them, what results did you find with those you visited?"

"Really good. Some had clearly trusted Christ, and others were definitely interested."

Making time for prayer had paid off. Seldom have I heard of ten percent of a student body turning out for an evangelistic activity, even a movie. And to have over three hundred give their name, with many making clear, first-time decisions, is remarkable. Promotion and preparation helped. But the Spirit of God worked, and much of the impact came from those two days a month taken out of busy schedules for fasting and prayer.

Extra Times

My wife and I also find it a spiritual boost to set apart extra times to be alone with the Lord—sometimes an hour, occasionally an evening, half a day, or even more. When possible, we get away from home to avoid distractions. Our favorite spot is the Botanic Gardens near downtown Singapore. Traffic rushes by a few yards away, and tourists troop past looking at the exotic foliage, but we feel isolated in this natural setting with no phone to answer, and no business to demand our attention.

First we spend time together in the Word and prayer, often using a special prayer list that we make up for the occasion. Then we usually separate and spend the remaining time alone with the Lord in the Word, prayer, praise, and reflection. Frequently we evaluate the recent past and plan for the coming week or month. Sometimes we feel richly rewarded, sometimes not. But we invest these times by faith and see results whether or not we feel them at the time.

As Christian workers, Ruth and I have more control over our schedules than many people do. Yet extra times with God are necessary for anyone convinced of the priority of prayer. Often this requires missing a desirable or important activity such as a visit with friends, reading a magazine, hearing a special speaker, an evening of television, or overtime at work.

A. W. Tozer portrayed a praying Christian as a constant threat to the stability of Satan's government. "The Christian is a holy rebel loose in the world with access to the throne of God," he wrote. "Satan never knows from what direction the danger will come."[6] Since prayer is lethal to his purposes, Satan does his utmost to interfere when we pray. He especially opposes us in this matter of taking time for prayer. He knows what it is going to cost him, so he fights us.

In spite of Satan's attempts to keep you from it, make time for prayer. Decide by faith to give prayer priority over activities. We can do more than pray after we have prayed, but we cannot do more than pray until we have prayed.

Give God Your Best Time

For daily time with the Lord, the quiet morning before the activities of the day begin seems uniquely blessed by God. In *Power Through Prayer* E. M. Bounds writes,

> The men who have done the most for God in this world have been early on their knees. He who fritters away the early morning, its opportunity and freshness, in other pursuits than seeking God will make poor headway seeking Him the rest of the day.[7]

The mere discipline of rising early has no special virtue, nor is God limited to meeting us only in the morning. Our afternoons and evenings, however, are easily eroded by unexpected activities that crowd out our intended quiet time, or we become too tired to enjoy His fellowship. The recognition that God is the most important person in my life, deserving first priority in my day, is of great consequence.

One way to demonstrate God's priority in our lives is to get to bed early enough to rise and meet our Father without dozing. The discipline of getting up starts the night before. I sometimes must deny myself the luxury of consuming an hour at night doing useful-but-secondary things—skimming a magazine, straightening my desk, lingering over a snack—when I should be preparing for that special appointment with God.

Numerous times I have fallen asleep on my knees while reading or praying. There is no spiritual merit in such sleep or in the aches that follow. And it is embarrassing when someone taps you on the shoulder to let you know breakfast is ready, or that the prayer meeting is over.

Some people function more effectively at night. For them, perhaps afternoons or evenings are best for their quiet times. "Let each man be fully convinced in his own mind" about what time is best for him.[8] If you have your longer time with God later in the day, take at least five minutes in the morning to commit yourself and your day to Him, and to fix your heart on some truth from the Scriptures. This could be from your favorite verse of the previous evening or from a few moments of Bible reading. Put your armor on before the battle begins, not after it ends.

Be Creative

The busier we are, the more ingenious we must be to find time for fellowship with God. I know men who commute to work, leaving home at 5 A.M. and returning in time for a late dinner. They use those long rides for reading, prayer, and reviewing Scripture verses, even when standing on a crowded bus. Others use a portion of their lunch hour for reading and prayer.

Busy mothers have a different problem, for small children often wake up early and need attention all day long. Some mothers have a quiet time when the children nap. Ruth Graham, wife of the famous evangelist Billy Graham, and mother of five children, kept several Bibles open around the house. She would find times during the day when she could pick up one of the Bibles for a few moments of fellowship with the Lord. This helped her focus her attention on Him as she proceeded with her work.

Many mothers find it helpful to copy verses on slips of paper or cards and tape them above the kitchen sink, on their bathroom mirror, or near the ironing board.

Susannah Wesley, mother of the great eighteenth-century evangelist and Christian leader John Wesley, had nineteen children. When she wanted to pray and meditate, she would sit in her rocking chair and cover her face with her apron. She trained her children to respect these times of quietness and fellowship with God.

These solutions may not be ideal, but they are creative and demonstrate a heart that *makes* time for Christ. In *The Practice of Prayer*, G. Campbell Morgan emphasizes the value of even a short quiet time:

Five minutes with Him in which the soul is touched by the forces of eternity will mean a day full of spiritual vigor. God can do much in five minutes of a man's time if no more can honestly be spared. He can do nothing in five minutes for the man who should give Him sixty, but who is slothful.[9]

We must jealously guard the time we set apart for the Lord and use it well. Give Him the best time you possibly can. Tune your heart to love Him, obey Him, and tell others about Him. Continually remind yourself, as James Gilmore reminded his readers, that God is waiting to answer your call.

Cannot the same wonders be done now as of old? . . . Oh that God would give me more practical faith in Him! Where is now the Lord God of Elijah? He is waiting for Elijah to call on Him.[10]

Personal Application
Ask the Lord if He wants you to make any adjustments in your schedule or your time with Him by answering these questions:
1. Are there any changes in my quiet time You want me to make?
2. Should I schedule an extra period of time for prayer this week?
3. Are there any pockets of time during the day I can use for prayer?

NOTES   1. *Kneeling We Triumph,* compiled by Edwin and Lillian Harvey (Moody Press, 1971), pages 34–35.
        2. S. D. Gordon, *Quiet Talks on Prayer* (Grosset and Dunlap, 1904), page 12.
        3. Psalm 127:1.
        4. Hebrews 11:6.
        5. Luke 5:15-16, 6:12.
        6. A. W. Tozer, *That Incredible Christian* (Christian Publications, Inc., 1964), page 71.
        7. E. M. Bounds, *Power Through Prayer* (Zondervan Publishing House, n.d.), page 42.
        8. Romans 14:5.
        9. G. Campbell Morgan, *The Practice of Prayer* (Fleming H. Revell Company, 1960), page 111.
      10. James Gilmour, as quoted by E. M. Bounds in *Purpose in Prayer* (Moody Press, n.d.), page 5.

16

Pray Anytime, Anywhere

I cannot tell why there should come to me
A thought of someone miles and years away
In swift insistence on the memory,
Unless there is a need that I should pray.
Perhaps just then my friend has fiercer fight,
A more appalling weakness, a decay
Of courage, darkness, some lost sense of right;
And so, in case he needs my prayers, I pray.
—Mrs. Jonathan Goforth,
Goforth of China

Often we remember incidents that happened years ago: our school days, a special friendship, a life-changing conference, a mistake or attitude we regret. Something in the present—a vaguely familiar face, a place, a situation, a dream—may bring to mind past events and people. Or we simply remember someone. How does God want us to use such thoughts?

Mrs. Goforth's poem motivates me to pray for friends and acquaintances who flash to mind though I may not have seen them for years. Are they still alive? Have they ever trusted Christ? Are they walking in victory? Do they have special needs? Assuming they are still living, I offer a brief prayer for their salvation or their spiritual progress. I pray on the spot wherever I am, for the flash of remembrance is quickly forgotten.

Short, concise prayers offered anytime, anywhere, are both scriptural and immensely useful. Nehemiah was a master of such prayers. While he was serving as cupbearer for Artaxerxes, ruler of the Persian Empire, he received the distressing news that the wall of Jerusalem had been broken down and the gates had been burned. Later, when King Artaxerxes unexpectedly asked Nehemiah to state his request regarding Jerusalem, he quickly "prayed to the God of heaven," then answered the King.[1] Later in Jerusalem, when enemies tried to frighten Nehemiah and his men to prevent them from rebuilding the city wall, his emergency prayer was, "But now, O God, strengthen my hands."[2] Nehemiah concluded his book with a brief cry to God that he often used, with variations: "Remember me, O my God, for good."[3]

Use Your Private Line
God never limits us to scheduled times for approaching Him. Every moment, twenty-four hours a day, we can boldly request mercy for our failures and find appropriate help just when we need it.[4] Each of us has a private line, an immediate connection that we can use without any preliminaries. The switchboard never gives us a busy signal, nor need we fear monopolizing God's time and crowding out someone else. The privilege of this private line is all the more remarkable when we realize that it connects us with the throne room of the universe.

LeRoy Eims, assistant to the president of The Navigators, tells of a woman he met on a plane. Upon discovering they were both from the same city and that LeRoy worked for The Navigators, she asked, "Do you happen to know . . .?"

"Yes, I know him well."

"Would you help me? Some weeks ago I met him, and he told me of his faith and encouraged me to believe in God personally. I wasn't interested, and what he said annoyed me. But as we parted, he told me he would pray for me, especially that God would make me miserable until I trusted Christ personally. Mr. Eims, I want you to do me a favor. Ever since I met him I have been completely miserable and I don't know what to do about it. Would you ask God to cancel that man's prayers?"

"Oh, no ma'am. I can't do that. He has a private line to heaven as all Christians do, and there is no way that I can cut in on him or cancel his requests. Besides, he didn't want you miserable, but was eager for you to experience the joy of Christ's fellowship."

We need more diligence in using our private line whenever

the Lord prompts us, whether for ourselves or others. Everything that concerns us interests Him. If a matter in any way occupies our mind or touches our emotions, we should pray about it. The great antidote for worry, weakness, frustration, and disappointment is to pray about everything.

Learning to pray about what comes to mind during the day helps develop the habit of praying without ceasing, as we're told to do in 1 Thessalonians 5:17. Sometimes a prayer is only a few seconds long. At other times we start with one brief request, and the Lord leads us on to pray for a number of things.

We can come anytime, in any place, with our bodies in any position—kneeling, sitting, standing, walking, or even jogging. I find it particularly profitable to pray during my morning runs.

Think of odd moments of the day when you could engage in brief prayers; for example, standing in line, walking between classes, riding in an elevator, or waiting for an appointment. Decide also on specific acts that will remind you to pray: leaving the house, beginning a new task, sealing a letter, or washing dishes.

Ruth and I find many spare minutes for prayer. Sometimes we pray in the kitchen while cleaning up after a meal, or in the bathroom while she is combing her hair and I am shaving. Often we pray while driving or traveling by bus or plane.

A young believer in Kenya, Africa, felt prayer invariably required a bowed head and closed eyes. One day while he was driving a Landrover, his companion suggested they pray. They ended up bouncing across a meadow. Though I usually pray with my eyes closed, I make an exception when I drive.

On long trips Ruth and I often begin by asking the Lord for safety and good judgment, perhaps including requests for our family, co-workers, and friends. Sometimes our praying leads us into profitable communicating with each other. At other times, we pray much of the way. Often upon reaching our destination we are surprised at how much we have covered in prayer and how satisfying it has been.

There are also times when we forget about praying until the end of our trip. A few minutes before arriving we remember to pray, but have little time to mention important concerns. We find the pray-as-you-start habit more satisfactory and fruitful.

Pause now and ask God that such specific activities will remind you to pray. Ask Him to teach your heart to pray while your hands and feet are busy.

Arrow Prayers Get Results

One of the shortest prayers recorded in the Bible is a three-word cry of desperation: "Lord, save me!" Peter had suddenly realized the total impossibility of walking on water. His faith faltered and he began to sink. At a time like that, a "proper prayer" with introductory phrases, eloquence, and careful grammar was inadvisable. Peter's arrow prayer was enough. Christ immediately reached out His hand and rescued His sinking apostle.[5]

We have had similar experiences with prayers which, like arrows quickly shot from a bow toward a target, are shot toward heaven for immediate help, guidance, or protection, or in response to special prompting.

Once in India we were in a taxi racing to Bombay's Santa Cruz Airport when it began to rain. As we approached a turn, an oil slick caused our taxi to skid toward people waiting at a bus stop. Like Peter, I had no time to say any more than, "Lord Jesus, take over!' Miraculously the taxi straightened out. Then it began to skid in the other direction toward a concrete wall. Again I shot an arrow prayer, "Jesus, take over, take over!" The trembling driver finally straightened out the taxi. Ruth and I, also shaken, rejoiced and praised God for His care and quick answers.

Not all arrow prayers are emergency cries for help. One evening while my wife, then a widow, was making dinner, she thought of her daughter Doreen's limited supply of blouses, and how often she had to wash and iron them. Ruth casually talked it over with God: "Father, Doreen doesn't have enough blouses to last all week. That's all right, but it would be nice to have more." Two days later the doorbell rang. There stood the postman with a package from a church in another state. In the package, which had been mailed several days before Ruth prayed, were blouses for Doreen plus two pairs of jeans for her brother, Brian. Though not included in the prayer, the jeans were also much needed. As the Lord states in Isaiah 65:24, "It will . . . come to pass that before they call, I will answer; and while they are still speaking, I will hear."

Frank Laubach, the great apostle of literacy, found that arrow prayers constantly tuned him in to God's guidance. He wrote,

> All during the day, in the chinks of time between the things we find ourselves obliged to do, there are moments when our minds ask: "What next?" In these chinks of time, ask Him: "Lord, think Thy thoughts in my mind. What is on Thy mind for me to do now?"
>
> When we ask Christ, "What next?" we tune in and give Him a chance to pour His ideas through our enkindled imagination. If we persist, it becomes a habit. It takes some effort, but it is worth a million times what it costs.[6]

We can use arrow prayers to intercede for others, even strangers. Many times when I pass a person on the street or see someone on a bus, the Lord prompts me to pray that the person might come to know Him or have a special need met. Though we seldom learn of specific answers to such prayers, God hears them.

One of my college friends, Virgil, a cheerleader at the University of California, came to know the Lord. Betty, a Christian who had passed out uniforms to men enrolling in university military training, heard of his conversion. Excitedly she told me how the Lord had specifically prompted her to pray for Virgil a few months before, as he and scores of others picked up their uniforms. She had prayed, "Lord, save this young man," and had given him little further thought. Probably Betty's arrow prayer was just one of the prayers that brought Virgil to know Christ, but it played a part.

The chain of influences that leads to a person's conversion has many links. Sometimes we are the first link as we witness or pray. Many times we are an unheralded middle link. Occasionally the Lord enables us to be the last link, helping the person make a decision to trust Christ. But who knows how many arrow prayers have helped form the chain?

With all the encouragement God gives us to pray, why do we neglect so many opportunities? I wonder if some day we will meet the Lord with the surprised comment, "But, Lord, if I had known You were going to answer all those tiny, casual prayers, I would have prayed more!"

Cultivating the Presence of God

Praying anywhere, anytime includes more than just making requests. It involves confessing as soon as we realize we have sinned, so that our fellowship with God is kept intact. It also involves praise and thanksgiving for God Himself, for the blessings He bestows, and for the events He allows in our lives. "In everything give thanks; for this is God's will for you in Christ Jesus."[7]

I find it liberating to develop the habit of thanking the Lord for little and big things throughout the day—pleasant and unpleasant things, problems and solutions. When I fail to do this, I frequently complain and become irritated.

Constant prayer involves a day-in and day-out interchange of thought with God. If a matter is the subject of our thinking, we can make it a subject of conversation with God, bringing Him into our thoughts as we would any close friend. Brother Lawrence, when asked why he felt prayer was important, replied, "We establish in ourselves a sense of God's presence by continually conversing with Him."

Bring God into your enjoyments. "Isn't that a breathtaking view, Lord!" "Father, isn't that a lovely child." ".What a delight, Lord, to have finished that project. Thank You for helping me."

Also bring Him into your doubts and failures. Discuss them with Him, ask for help and guidance, and thank Him that He promises to weave them together for the good of all concerned. "Lord, I made a mess of that situation. Thank You that You can use it for good. What should I do *now*?"

Moment-by-moment praying keeps our confidence centered in God. Consciously relying on God can keep us from unconsciously relying on ourselves. The secret uplifting of our hearts to depend on God does not mean we will become "so heavenly minded that we are of no earthly good." Ruth and I have found that bringing God into our activities and thoughts greatly increases our earthly effectiveness, our enjoyment of life, and our peace of mind.

Throughout the day our mind is occupied with a flow of thoughts. These thoughts fluctuate from the useful (planning, studying, concentrating on a conversation) to the idle (daydreaming, letting our minds wander) to the harmful (mental arguments, worries, complaints, lustful fantasies). God wants us to redirect this natural undercurrent of thoughts, and has implanted His Spirit in ours to renew our mind and help us focus it on things above.[8] Through His power we can pray and meditate on God's Word more consistently.

This new flow of thoughts brings a delightful companionship with God in which we listen to Him and speak to Him throughout our waking hours. It takes us beyond occasional *acts* of prayer and even a regular *habit* of prayer into a *life* of prayer, in which our thoughts are directed toward God. Frank Laubach believes we need to "acquire a new way of thinking. Thinking is a process of talking to your 'inner self.' Instead of talking to yourself, talk to the invisible Christ."[9]

Although we cannot consciously think of God at every moment, we can bring Him into everything, including complicated tasks or knotty problems that demand intense concentration. And as the Spirit controls and molds our mind, it becomes like the indicator on a scale: when no weight is present, it automatically points upward.

Practical Helps

The habit of constant prayer is not developed quickly. We cannot simply decide to pray without ceasing and suddenly do it. All of us need growth in this.

One aid to continual conversation with God is memorizing His Word. As we find verses that turn our eyes to the Lord or motivate us to obey, we can make them ours by memorizing and meditating on them. Then they serve as built-in speakers through which God can talk to us in special ways throughout the day. In response we can talk to Him further about the meaning and application of the verses and can use them in prayer for ourselves and others. God's Word in our hearts helps us hear Him speak as well as converse with Him.

Another help is to formulate a basic prayer that becomes our special arrow prayer for the present period of our life, a prayer we use repeatedly to turn our hearts to God. Here are examples.

Lord, I choose to be joyful and confident right now, because Christ is my life and You are in control of my circumstances.

I can do all things through Christ who infuses inner strength into me.[10]

The Lord God omnipotent reigns, in His universe and in me. Hallelujah!

Make up a prayer and use it to increase your confidence in God and deepen your friendship with Him.

By praying anytime, anywhere, we allow God to be our steady companion. Prayer should become the key of the morning as we get out of bed, the bolt at night as we fall asleep, and the breath of our in-between hours.

Personal Application
1. Which of my daily activities can I now begin to use as a reminder to pray?
2. Which of the suggestions on pages 121–122 can I start using to develop the habit of constant prayer?

NOTES
1. Nehemiah 2:4.
2. Nehemiah 6:9.
3. Nehemiah 13:31.
4. Hebrews 4:16, AMP.
5. Matthew 14:28–31.
6. Frank Laubach, as quoted in *Kneeling We Triumph*, compiled by Edwin and Lillian Harvey (Moody Press, 1971), page 74.
7. 1 Thessalonians 5:18.
8. Colossians 3:2.
9. Laubach.
10. Based on Philippians 4:13, AMP.

17

Keep On Asking

> The great point is to never give up until the answer comes. *I have been praying for fifty-two years, every day for two men, sons of a friend of my youth. They are not converted yet, but they will be! . . . The great fault of the children of God is, they do not continue in prayer; they do not go on praying; they do not persevere. If they desire anything for God's glory, they should pray until they get it.*
> —George Mueller

In chapters five through nine we studied the first of Christ's three teachings on prayer in Luke eleven—the prayer Jesus taught His disciples, which serves as a pattern for us to follow. Christ's second great teaching on prayer emphasizes persistence, or importunity. Persistence could also be translated "shamelessness" or "shameless persistence." It does not mean irreverently demanding what we want, but asking repeatedly with bold confidence. This may mean praying for many days or many years. Jesus Christ gave a parable to illustrate this aspect of prayer.

> And He said to them, "Suppose one of you shall have a friend, and shall go to him at midnight, and say to him, 'Friend, lend me three loaves; for a friend of mine has come to me from a journey, and I have nothing to set before him'; and from inside he shall answer and say, 'Do not bother me; the door has already been shut and my children and I are in bed; I cannot get up and give you anything'¹

Even in modern society, a friend knocking at midnight deserves an answer, and the demands of hospitality were greater in the ancient East. But there were also the demands of family. One room served as bedroom, living room, workshop, and possibly kitchen. Parents and children probably slept on mats on the floor. The front door was locked and barred, and opening it at midnight would have disturbed the whole family. Family considerations prevailed, and the visiting friend perhaps heard a sleepy reply: "I'm in bed. My wife is in bed. My children are in bed. We're all trying to sleep! Come back tomorrow!"

I can envision the visitor's response. He was not obnoxious; he did not blaspheme or shout insults or kick the door. The passage implies that he just continued knocking. Perhaps the wife stirred and asked, "What's happening?" The children started to cry. The neighbors on one side began to murmur, then the neighbors on the other side.

Sensing family and public relations problems on the horizon, the grumbling householder said, "Just a minute good friend, just a minute," as he climbed over his family, unbolted the door, gave a curt greeting, and stumbled to the cupboard, trying his sleepy best not to step on anyone's hand or foot or face. He returned to the door with the loaves, saying, "This is all the bread we have, but take it and keep any extra for other friends who might visit you tonight. Go in peace." And with a gentle push he bade his friend good night.

Christ states the application of the parable in verses nine and ten:

> So I say to you, _Ask and keep on asking_, and it shall be given you; _seek and keep on seeking_, and you shall find; _knock and keep on knocking_, and the door shall be opened to you. For everyone who asks and keeps on asking receives, and he who seeks and keeps on seeking finds, and to him who knocks and keeps on knocking the door shall be opened.[2]

Persistence in prayer does not mean overcoming God's reluctance or annoying God until He gives in. It means continuing with unashamed confidence to request what we know is His will, even though the answer is delayed.

Why Persistence?

I used to wonder why I should bring a request to God two, ten, or a hundred times. Was not once enough? We may also wonder, "Why ask God even once? Why pray at all, since He knows our needs even before we tell Him?" We ask, and we ask with persistence, not because we understand all the reasons, but because Jesus Christ taught us to pray in this way.

I have heard people say, "If you have faith, it is only necessary to ask God once." True, answers often do come quickly. And sometimes when the answer is not immediate, the Holy Spirit gives such special confidence, such assurance about an answer, that from then on we merely praise the Lord for what He is going to do.

Nevertheless Jesus taught us to persist in prayer. Whether through continued praise or continued asking, we must remind God persistently about many of our requests—day after day, week after week, year after year—until the answer comes. Both the Scriptures and the great men of prayer throughout the centuries have emphasized the importance of such persistence.

Why has God made prayer, and often persistent prayer, a requirement for receiving His benefits? Is it that we must make Him more desirous of blessing us? No, God longs to give us good things. But He longs for more. He wants an intimate, communicating relationship with us in which we love and seek Him, a relationship characterized by a childlike dependence and a thankful spirit. And He wants to enrich us with something infinitely more valuable than the specific gifts we request—a rich personal experience of Himself.

Many of us would bypass these deeper blessings of dependence and fellowship if the Lord automatically provided all our needs without our asking, or with our asking only once. God foresaw this and planned accordingly. He made prayer not an optional luxury but a prescribed way for us to receive His blessings. Our needs and desires spur us to draw near to Him rather than neglect Him. And as we pray and wait and keep on praying, we receive the eventual answers with a deeper experience of His presence and goodness.

Persistent prayer does not change God's will, but it is often

His way of accomplishing His will, and it does change us. Delayed answers that require persistence help us grow. They increase our trust in God, as we come to Him again and again and see the perfect timing of His answers and His faithfulness. They develop our perseverance and our character and help us overcome impatience. Especially if answers are long delayed, our impatience surfaces, causing us to question God or complain about His ways and timing. Richard C. Halverson wrote,

> One may sin—not by what he does but by refusing to *wait*.
> Wanting a good thing is virtuous, wanting a good thing *now* may
> be sin. Impatience indicates a lack of trust in the perfection of
> God's will and way.[3]

Continued praying can help us relax and wait for God's perfect time and plan. And should the request need modifying, this becomes obvious *as* we wait and pray. The delay enables us to clarify or redirect our petition.

We are to pray persistently, not to change God's will, but to see it done. We pray not to overcome God's unwillingness, but because God has ordained prayer as His appointed way to provide and act for us. If we fail to pray, we cause Him to withhold many of the blessings He longs to bestow.

Persistence or Repetition?

People sometimes wonder how persistent prayers fit with Matthew 6:7, which warns against being repetitious as the heathen are. In many non-Christian religions, the name of a god or a brief prayer is repeated hundreds of times a day, with the belief that mentioning the god's name or saying the magical sentence builds up merit or obtains answers. Some years ago *Time* magazine told of a man who had decided to repeat the Lord's prayer three thousand times a day to bring world peace. Either he stopped too soon or had the wrong formula, for a later issue of *Time* reported that twenty-eight wars were currently in progress.

Jesus warns against empty, useless repetitions. They differ vastly from thoughtful, meaningful repetition based on the Word of God. Bold and patient persistence is taught by Jesus Christ, emphasized in other Scriptures,[4] and has been proven in the lives of the great men of prayer, as well as in our own experience.

Persistence Rewarded

The Lord works in notable ways through persistent prayer.

Some years ago in Singapore, a teenage neighbor, Angeline, came to our home for an evening of special music and a discussion about Christ. She then attended a Bible study for a few weeks. Though I did not talk with her after that, I prayed for her salvation several times a week as I jogged by her house in the early morning.

Recently in church a young woman greeted us by saying, "Hello. I'm Angeline, your neighbor."

"Oh, are you Mr. Koh's daughter?"

"That's right. I'm now twenty-one, and my mother has given me permission to be baptized and join the church."

"Wonderful. When did you trust Christ personally, and how did it happen?"

"About two years ago through the help of a friend and the church."

Perhaps because she had shown a spiritual interest a few years earlier, and perhaps just through the Lord's prompting, I made Angeline a focus of continued prayer for years. And God answered.

Earlier the son of another neighbor trusted Christ after we prayed for him for several years. For others on the street, we continue to pray and witness and wait.

For three years I prayed almost daily for a forthcoming planning conference the Lord laid on my heart. Frequently, I prayed for it more than once a day, either with my wife, with a friend, or alone. During the conference, we were particularly conscious that the Lord was in control. We accomplished far more than we had expected, and the Lord gave clarity and unity that come only from His Spirit.

George Mueller often received immediate and dramatic answers to his requests. One night at bedtime, when the pantry was empty, he prayed that God would provide breakfast for two thousand orphans. The Lord answered in a surprising way, and the children ate in abundance at the usual hour the next morning.

One time, while crossing the Atlantic to Canada, and not wanting to be late for an engagement, he astounded the ship's captain by praying away a dense, persistent fog.[5]

Yet this remarkable man also practiced persistence in prayer. Sometimes he waited for weeks, months, or years for answers. Often his faith was severely tested. But when he knew a request was God's will, he would continue to pray daily, or several times a day, until the answer came. He did not interpret delays as denials.

> I once asked a thing of God, which I knew to be according to His mind, and though I brought it day by day *and generally many times a day* before Him, in such assurance as to be able to thank Him hundreds of times for the answer before it was received, yet I had to wait three years and ten months before the blessing was given to me (italics mine).[6]

George Mueller's answers to prayer, financial and otherwise, were often spectacular. Ours, though less dramatic, have caused Ruth and me to praise God and rejoice at His provision many times.

Month by month during a recent year we fell short financially. We re-evaluated our needs and economized, but mainly we prayed. We focused prayer primarily on the yearly goal, reminding the Lord almost daily of our need. The Lord kept us from having to curtail our ministry, and by the end of the year we had reached our financial goal with a few dollars to spare.

Many times we have had similar answers for monthly needs and for special projects. God is wonderfully faithful and able, and is eager for His children to determine His will, persist in prayer, and trust Him for the right time and answer.

Another subject of persistent prayer is for God to work in the lives of Christians. I find this requires more diligence and perseverance than does praying for material needs, since progress usually appears a little at a time. But God rewards Spirit-led persistence as we pray for others and for ourselves.

We have seen this in our son and daughter as they have been delivered from Satan's snares, have put Christ first in their lives, and have married stable, spiritual partners. Our son has been lifted out of prolonged doubts and despair in answer to the persistent prayers of many. We have also prayed repeatedly for others and have seen the Lord answer in guiding, using, and protecting them.

Persevering prayer and answers are the result of God's grace and leading, plus our persistent cooperation. His is the large part ✓ and ours the small, but both parts are essential.

In Luke 18 Christ again teaches the principle of persistence in prayer. In the first verse He states the lesson we are to learn: *people should persevere in prayer* in order to keep from becoming discouraged and giving up. He teaches that if an unrighteous judge answers a widow's pleading because of her persistence, how much more will our just and loving God answer His people who cry to Him time after time. Jesus is not likening God's character to that of the unjust judge. His point is that we should pray as persistently as if we were dealing with an unjust judge.

If we are asking anything for God's glory, we should pray until He answers. Such persistence is essential to a scriptural and effective prayer life. How necessary it is that people "should always pray and not give up."[7]

Personal Application

1. What two requests—one for myself and one for someone else—should I begin to ask God for?
2. What can I do to help myself pray regularly for these needs?

NOTES   1. Luke 11:5–8.
            2. AMP, italics mine.
            3. Richard C. Halverson, *Somehow Inside of Eternity* (Zondervan Publishing House, 1978), page 42.
            4. Isaiah 62:6–7, Ephesians 1:15–16, Colossians 1:9 and 4:12.
            5. See the appendix for a full account of these two experiences.
            6. Robert Steer, *George Mueller: Delighted in God* (London: Hodder and Stoughton, 1975), page 266.
            7. Luke 18:1, NIV.

18

Depend on the Holy Spirit

> The Spirit must be honored not
> only as the Author of a new life
> but also as the Leader and
> Director of our entire walk . . .
> Let us not be satisfied with
> anything less than hearty
> surrender to and undivided
> appropriation of the Spirit.
> —Andrew Murray,
> The Prayer Life

Luke 11:11–13 is the third of Christ's teachings on prayer.

> Now suppose one of you fathers is asked by his son for a fish; he
> will not give him a snake instead of a fish, will he? Or if he is
> asked for an egg, he will not give him a scorpion, will he? If you
> then, being evil, know how to give good gifts to your children,
> how much more shall your heavenly Father give the Holy Spirit to
> those who ask Him?

In Matthew 7:9, Christ asks another question: "Or what man is
there among you, when his son shall ask him for a loaf, will give
him a stone?" When does a child ask for a fish, an egg, or especially bread? Whenever he is hungry. Perhaps several times a day:
mid-morning, after school, just before dinner, perhaps before he
goes to bed as well. Fish, eggs, and bread are relatively common
foods in many parts of the world; they are not special foods to be
served only at parties or on holidays. A child asks for such food
whenever he needs it.

Christ is teaching that this is how we should ask for the Holy

Spirit—whenever we are aware of our need for Him.

Do we need love for others? We should ask, for the fruit of the Spirit is love.

Do we need encouragement and hope? The Holy Spirit is the Encourager, and through His power our lives can overflow with hope.[1]

Are we suddenly tempted to exhibit an unscriptural attitude toward someone? We can send up a quick arrow prayer such as, "Lord, give me the attitude You want me to have!"

Do we need help as we witness? One of His special ministries is to empower us as His witnesses and to convince men of sin because they do not believe in Christ.[2] We should ask for the Holy Spirit to do this as we witness.

Do we need understanding of a portion of Scripture? We should pray, and in His time the Spirit will teach us.

Do we need a deeper and warmer fellowship with God and His Son? His Spirit wants to bring this about.

Do we need help in prayer? The Spirit of supplication will guide and empower us as we pray.

As many times a day as we are conscious of our need of the Holy Spirit's help and fullness, we should ask for it. He is the Teacher God has provided so that we can know and enjoy the riches God has freely given us. He is our Encourager, Comforter, Counselor, and Helper. He lives in us and is eager to meet our needs as we pray for His help.

The Fullness of the Spirit

When a person receives Jesus Christ as his personal Savior, he receives forgiveness, eternal life, and the Holy Spirit.[3] Every true Christian has been born of the Spirit, sealed by the Spirit, and baptized by the Spirit into the body of Christ.[4] Each one is indwelt by the Spirit.[5] We need not ask for these things even as we need not pray repeatedly that we will be born spiritually, or become God's children, or be made heirs of God. All these things happened the moment we trusted the Lord Jesus Christ as our Savior.

It is for the other ministries of the Holy Spirit that we should pray, the ones we need continually *after* being born again spiritually. These ministries are closely related to letting the Holy

Spirit continually fill us, as Ephesians 5:18 commands: "Be filled with the Spirit." The Holy Spirit is the living water Jesus gave us to drink when we were born again. When we drink physical water, it quenches our thirst and is carried throughout our body to meet its needs. The Holy Spirit, along with the Word He inspired, is the spiritual water through which the Lord meets our spiritual and emotional needs.

The Spirit dwells in our inner man as an artesian well, "springing up to eternal life."[6] He wants to fill our personality much as fresh water keeps filling and saturating a riverbed. "He who believes in Me, as the Scripture said, 'From his innermost being shall flow rivers of living water.' "[7]

To be filled with the Spirit is to let Him guide and empower us and accomplish His gracious ministries in us. As we yield moment by moment to the Lord Jesus Christ and trust His sufficiency, the Holy Spirit controls us and liberates us to follow our true desires to love, obey, and glorify God. He restrains our tendencies to sin, reveals Christ to us, and transforms us more and more into the glorious beings God intends us to be.[8]

Evidences of being filled by the Spirit are a singing heart, a thankful heart, and a submissive, obedient, considerate heart in our daily relationships.[9] In Galatians 5:22–23 Paul refers to further evidences of the fullness of the Holy Spirit as "the fruit of the Spirit."

In requesting the Spirit's filling, we can simply say, "Lord, if this hour depends on me, it will be a failure. I ask You to fill, empower, and control me by Your Spirit, giving strength and victory"—or love, wisdom, power, patience, purity—whatever our specific need is. As followers of Christ, we need not beg the Father to fill us with the Spirit, but simply pray, choosing to believe that the Holy Spirit will lead and enable us. He is eager to work in us and through us to glorify the Lord. This is why He indwells us.

If you find any of the teachings in Luke 11 hard to understand or apply, you have an opportunity to pray for the Holy Spirit to teach you and to confirm the truths in your own experience. Bring your questions to Him repeatedly, and be alert for answers in His Word or through others. But do not wait for total understanding before you apply His teachings and pray. Prayer is an act of faith. It is a response to the clear teaching of God, with or without full comprehension or a complete theology of prayer. Prayer is an indispensable part of Christlike living and serving.

Prayer Is Hard Work

In his book *Spiritual Leadership* J. Oswald Sanders wrote, "Both our Lord and His bondslave Paul made it clear that true praying is not pleasant, dreamy reverie. 'All vital praying makes a drain on a man's vitality,' wrote J. H. Jowett."[10]

Recognizing that prayer is hard work has brought me new freedom. It releases me from unrealistic expectations that prayer will get easier. It helps me give myself to this essential of the Christian life, even though it takes concentration and energy. Lorne Sanny has said,

> Prayer will never be easy. It is harder for me to pray now than ten years ago. I thought I would reach the place where I couldn't keep from praying. Instead I can hardly keep from not praying. Why should it be easy? It is warfare.

Epaphras, one of Paul's close colaborers, also found that prayer requires effort: "Epaphras, who is one of you and a servant of Christ Jesus, sends greetings. He is always *wrestling in prayer* for you, that you may stand firm in all the will of God, mature and fully assured. I vouch for him that he is *working hard* for you."[11]

Epaphras labored in prayer with realistic expectations. He believed that his mighty God could change people. He believed that even while absent he could, through prayer, have a powerful ministry in the lives of his friends back in the Colossian church. He did not expect to see miracles of growth in people's lives through casual, on-and-off praying. He was willing to give himself to the hard work of wrestling in prayer. But he did not find such prayer easy.

Epaphras gave himself to prayer, asking the Lord that the Colossian believers would live mature lives and be certain about the will of God. Perhaps his love for the people at Colossae made this toil emotionally satisfying; but regardless of his feelings, he labored in prayer for them.

In any endeavor, hard work can be enjoyable. But we can

miss the enjoyment of prayer by depending on our own abilities. As we labor in prayer we must consciously depend on the Spirit for both direction and strength.

The Mystery of Prayer

Prayer is a paradox. The balance between depending upon the Holy Spirit and hard work on our part is similar to the broader balance between grace and works. The secret of victorious living, effective service, *and productive prayer* is always a combination of God's grace and our labor. Both are indispensable. Neither is sufficient by itself. Like two blades of a scissors or two wings of a bird, both parts must work together. Paul's life was a continual blend of God's grace and Paul's labor.

Nehemiah understood the need for both God's grace and man's labor when the enemy was threatening to stop the rebuilding of Jerusalem's wall. "But we prayed to our God and posted a guard day and night to meet this threat."[12] Where was Nehemiah's faith? Why post a guard if God was protecting the laborers? Was not prayer sufficient? God heard and did protect them, but it was also His will for His men to work with Him.

In prayer, as in our service, we must exert ourselves; yet without Christ we can do nothing.[13] Without His motivation and direction, all our effort is self-effort and produces nothing in eternal results.

Thus we live with seeming contradictions. However dimly we may understand it, our efforts and our prayers work together to affect people and events in this world and bear fruit for eternity. The Holy Spirit, reinforcing our human spirit, prompts and energizes us as we *make* time and give ourselves to the rewarding labor of prayer.

Colossians 4:2 could be paraphrased, "Persevere and don't be weary in prayer. *Give yourselves wholeheartedly to it.* Be alert both to needs and opportunities, and pray with thanksgiving." Although obeying this command involves work, such exertion need not become a boring routine or require tedious submission. God's commands are not like the barked orders of a drill sergeant, which we privates cannot escape.

God's commandments always offer us something good. This

is particularly true of His commands to pray. They offer us the privilege and freedom of direct, personal partnership with the Ruler of the universe. He does not intend our praying to be a crushing responsibility, but a way of making all our responsibilities lighter. Prayer demands perseverance but provides refreshment as well as answers. Viewed in true perspective, prayer is a burden to us only as wings are to an airplane or paddles are to a canoe.

So prayer remains a mystery. Scriptural prayer is a blending of the Holy Spirit's power with our faith and labor. It expends our vitality, yet brings us His renewing strength. Day by day we will find, as Dawson Trotman expressed it, "Truly our most difficult work—refreshing and wonderful as it is—is prayer."

Personal Application

1. What did the Lord impress on me in this chapter?
2. What should I do about this impression?

NOTES
1. Romans 15:13.
2. Acts 1:8, John 16:8–9.
3. John 1:12, Acts 10:43, Romans 8:9.
4. John 3:3–7, Ephesians 1:13, 1 Corinthians 12:13.
5. 1 Corinthians 3:16.
6. John 4:14.
7. John 7:38.
8. 2 Corinthians 3:17-18.
9. Ephesians 5:18-6:10.
10. J. Oswald Sanders, *Spiritual Leadership* (Moody Press, 1967), page 78.
11. Colossians 4:12-13, NIV.
12. Nehemiah 4:9, NIV.
13. John 15:5.

19

Pray for the Lost

> I urge, then, first of all, that
> requests, prayers, intercession
> and thanksgiving be made for
> everyone. . . . This is good, and
> pleases God our Savior, who
> wants all men to be saved and to
> come to a knowledge of the truth.
> For there is one God and one
> mediator between God and
> men—the man Christ Jesus, who
> gave Himself as a ransom
> for all men.
> (1 Timothy 2:1, 3–6, NIV).

Paul writes, "I urge that prayers be made for everyone." Praying for everyone includes our friends and loved ones. It includes fellow Christians and laborers in the spiritual harvest fields. It also includes the lost. We must pray for the lost because God urges us to pray for all people so that many will be saved and released from their bondage. "And what pity [Christ] felt for the crowds that came, because their problems were so great and they didn't know what to do or where to go for help. They were like sheep without a shepherd."[1]

God wants us to look beyond our own interests and our own circle of friends. A good place to begin is with the people we meet daily—people whose problems are so great that they don't know what to do or where to go for help. They are alienated from God and in the grip of forces too great for them to resist.

Other translations of Matthew 9:36 say that people are "bewildered and miserable," "harassed and helpless," even "mangled and thrown to the ground."

In a field just outside a village in Vietnam, a tiger attacked a

133

man. With its powerful jaws the huge beast dragged the man, alive and screaming, toward the jungle. At the edge of the clearing the tiger released its victim. As the man began to crawl away, the tiger grabbed him and pulled him back. Again and again it released and recaptured its victim, playing with him as a cat plays with a mouse, eventually dragging him off into the jungle.

Satan treats his victims in the same way, sometimes knocking them out with a single blow, sometimes toying with them through years of progressive bondage and misery, keeping them harassed and helpless, with "nothing to look forward to and no God" to whom they can turn.[2]

A Heart of Love and Concern

Christ asks us to open our eyes and see such people: our family, our neighbors, those with whom we work or study, and our casual contacts. Often they wear a smile and keep up a front of contentment and purpose, but inside they ache. Some are considering divorce. Some wish they had the courage for suicide but are afraid of what follows death. They dread living, and they fear dying. Many have problems and frustrations for which they see no answers. They are shepherdless, helpless, miserable, and repeatedly harassed until Satan, as a devouring lion, carries them off to be his forever.

Occasionally they take off their masks and share their deep inner struggles. At other times we can guess what their needs are by their unguarded words and actions. No matter how people appear or what they claim, without Christ they exist without His forgiveness and peace. They live in the dark and will die in the dark, to spend eternity as they spent their lives.

We are the privileged ones. By God's provision we have the light of life and need not stumble in the dark. We are no longer bound but liberated. We know the good news of the reconciled life and of the victorious life, and God holds us responsible to share this news with others. He wants us to see them, to empathize with them, and to labor and pray for their salvation.

[God] has reconciled us to Himself through Jesus Christ . . . *and has commissioned us with the message of reconciliation. We are now Christ's ambassadors,* as though God were appealing directly to you through us. *As his personal representatives we say, "Make your peace with God."*[3]

Often we fail Him. We refuse to accept our responsibility, we don't know how to get started, or we miss opportunities. Prayer is part of the solution for our failures—prayer that God will help us to see the lost as He sees them, and feel His pity and compassion for them; and prayer that we will choose to respond whether we feel moved or not.

Begin by praying over the Scriptures that describe man's lost condition, asking God to let you see people's true spiritual state. To accept the fact that members of our loving family, or many of our nice neighbors, or our kind and honest associates are spiritually lost and doomed requires faith. Our minds and emotions may say "No!" or "Why?" or "I don't think God will let anyone go to hell." But God says, "He who believes in the Son has eternal life; but he who does not obey the Son shall not see life, but the wrath of God abides on him."[4] "He will bring full justice in dazzling flame upon those who have refused to recognize God or to obey the Gospel of our Lord Jesus Christ. Their punishment will be eternal exclusion from the radiance of the face of the Lord, and the glorious majesty of his power."[5]

Begin to pray consistently for the lost, following Paul's example as he interceded for his lost countrymen: "My heart's desire and prayer to God for the Israelites is that they may be saved."[6] Part of Christ's Great Commission was to pray, and part was to go and proclaim His salvation. Only by doing both can we accomplish our mission of liberation.

Pause now and tell the Lord that you want to share His concern for the lost, which led Him to the cross, and that you want to labor with Him in prayer for people who need Him.

Pray for Specific People

By praying regularly for a few people, you can begin to focus the mighty weapon of prayer on lost men and women. Asking God to guide you, select several family members, neighbors, colleagues at work, or friends. Start with a few names and gradually add others. Do not be so ambitious that you get discouraged. Rather than trust your memory, make a list of the people for whom God leads you to intercede.

Pray daily for their salvation and for opportunities to speak to them. Though answers may not come quickly, persist in prayer, asking the Lord to break down inner barriers by His love and to convict them of sin by His Spirit. You can pray long prayers or short prayers as the Spirit leads, but the important thing is to pray regularly.

When I was attending the University of California, two friends and I met several times a week to pray for three unsaved men in our fraternity. We agreed also to send up quick arrow prayers for these three men every hour on the hour while we were on campus, each time the Campanile chimed the end of a class.

One of the three seemed totally indifferent, although he owned a Bible and had a Christian mother. When I talked to him about Christ, he let me know he was not interested. Years later, while overseas, I received a letter from this man saying, "Warren, I have discovered that the things you talked to me about ten years ago were right." When I returned to the United States, I found he had come to know Christ as his Savior through reading the Bible on his own. I had long before stopped praying for him daily, but God answered those early prayers. He might have received Christ sooner had I continued to persist in prayer.

The second man trusted Christ personally several months after we began to pray. I have never heard if the third man, now dead, responded to the Gospel.

Throughout the years the Lord keeps bringing to mind former high school, college, and Air Force friends. I keep lists and pray for some of them every day. Many of them I have not been able to contact for a personal witness, but I can pray.

In praying for unbelievers, we are not asking God to force them to come to Christ. God does not force people to make spiritual choices. In His sovereign will, He has chosen to allow them the freedom to either receive or to reject Him. Since none of us can pray effectively for very many of the people in the world, we should ask God to lay on our hearts the ones for whom He wants us to pray. When He gives us freedom and faith to keep lifting them to Him, we can confidently proceed, assured that we are helping to accomplish His eternal purposes.

As we pray, God works in people's lives to win them—sometimes in ways we would never have imagined and perhaps would not have chosen, especially when our loved ones are involved. He brings men and women to see their need, to hear and understand the Gospel, and to respond in faith.

Take a few moments now to pray for three people about whom you are concerned. Ask God to help you in the days ahead to be consistent in praying for them, and for others who need His salvation. Spirit-led, believing prayer is one of God's mighty weapons that can "break down every proud argument against God and every wall that can be built to keep men from finding Him."[7] Paul E. Billheimer writes,

> By means of persistent, believing intercession [we] may so release the Spirit of God upon a soul that he will find it easier to yield to the Spirit's tender wooing and be saved than to continue his rebellion.[8]

Personal Application

1. What practical steps can I take to pray more consistently for the lost?
2. Who should I begin to pray daily for?

NOTES
1. Matthew 9:36, *The Living Bible.*
2. Ephesians 2:12, PH.
3. 2 Corinthians 5:18–20, PH (italics mine).
4. John 3:36.
5. 2 Thessalonians 1:8–9, PH.
6. Romans 10:1, NIV.
7. 2 Corinthians 10:5, *The Living Bible.*
8. Paul E. Billheimer, *Destined for the Throne* (Christian Literature Crusade, 1975), page 17.

Develop a Global Vision

God loves our world—our lost world of men and women without Jesus Christ. He loves it so greatly that He sent His Son to be the light of the world, and to sacrifice Himself for the sins of the world. He wants the gospel preached in all the world, and has commissioned us to teach the entire truth to all the nations of the world.

God is interested in each one of the several billion people who live on the earth. That is why Jesus said, "I tell you, open your eyes and look at the fields! They are ripe for harvest. . . . The field is the world."[1] God wants His concerns to grip our hearts. How can this happen?

Become Informed
Throughout the Bible God uses facts to motivate people to accomplish His purposes. One way we can "look at the fields" is to get information about needs, not only in our church and neighborhood, our city and country, but also in other countries.

In your city, what people or groups are particularly fruitful

DEVELOP A GLOBAL VISION

in evangelism and in building effective believers? If they put out a newsletter or other publication, ask them to put you on their mailing list, and pray along with them. As you have opportunity, do the same with Christian works and workers in more distant places.

Begin by praying for laborers in one foreign country, becoming familiar with facts about it and with its needs. List requests on a prayer page, leaving room for any answers you learn of. Recording requests and answers reminds us to pray and provides a record for praise. As the Lord leads, adopt a second country, then a third.

When a newsletter particularly stimulates me, I use it in my quiet time or day of prayer. With some letters I pray immediately for one or two items. With other letters I put a few requests on a temporary prayer page, for further prayer. In addition, Ruth and I use newsletters for times of family prayer, for prayer at mealtimes, and for group prayer.

Although receiving too many publications and newsletters can be a burden, well-selected ones help us travel to places near and far by prayer. We can spend strategic minutes each day or half-hours each week in distant places at no cost and with no danger, investing our most valuable assets—ourselves, our time, and our prayers. S. D. Gordon describes prayer as "partnership with God in His planet-sized purposes," and suggests that we become agents in His secret service:

> The greatest thing each one of us can do is to pray. If we can go personally to some distant land, still we have gone to only one place.[2]
>
> Prayer puts us into direct dynamic touch with a world. A man may go aside today, and shut the door, and as really spend a half-hour of his life in India for God as though he were there in person. Surely you and I must get more half-hours for this secret service.[3]

Become Involved

Besides praying for spiritual needs in several places in the world, we can help alleviate physical needs through prayer. Prayer should not be a substitute for personal involvement or for sharing our abundance, for God also calls us to serve and give. As we have opportunity, we are to "do good to all people, especially to those who belong to the family of believers."[4] Prayer is a form of service and should precede our personal involvement and giving—prayer for guidance, love, and power as we reach out to others.

None of us can meet all the deep needs in this aching world. We must be selective. Which need should I be involved in? Which neighbor or family? Which situation? Which countries should I pray for? Ask the One who promises to make your way perfect to show you what His will is. He calls you to be a witness and a light. Let Him show you when and where and how. Thomas R. Kelly wrote,

> We cannot keep the love of God to ourselves. It spills over. . . . But in our love of people are we to be excitedly, hurriedly sweeping all men and tasks into our loving concern? No, that is God's function. But He, working within us, portions out his vast concern into bundles and lays on each of us our portion. These become our tasks.[5]

Pray for guidance that your service will be as broad as God desires, yet no broader. Pray also for effectiveness. How can we assure that whatever we do in word or deed is done in the name of the Lord Jesus?[6] How can we make certain that our witness will go forth in power, in the Holy Spirit, and with deep conviction?[7] How can we give wisely and in love? We can help guarantee these things through prayer. As we pray, God puts on our hearts our personal responsibilities, and we allow Him to be responsible for the timing and the results.

Only work done with God's guidance and strength will glorify Him and be permanent. Therefore pray as Moses did: "Let Thy work appear unto thy servants . . . and give permanence to the work of our hands; yes, give permanence to the work of our hands."[8]

Pray Creatively
In praying for the world, be resourceful and exercise faith.

One couple in South India moved to a new community in

order to proclaim Christ by life and by word. They were the only Christians among 300 deeply religious families strongly opposed to Christianity.

The first year was difficult. People were uninterested and unfriendly. Even casual conversation was hard. Utterly dependent on a faithful, powerful God, the couple prayed. Sometimes at night they would walk around their community, praying for each house and any individuals they knew.

But it was not convenient to do this every night, especially when the monsoon rains came. So they pasted a hand-drawn map of the community on the inside of their bedroom door. This "aerial-view" enabled them to walk through the neighborhood without leaving their house, praying for specific families and individuals.

Their diligent prayers began to produce results. One Christmas they showed an outdoor movie on the life of Christ. Many of the neighbors and all of the children came. A few effective colaborers infiltrated the crowd and started conversations.

One teenage boy, Kumar, made a decision to trust Christ. At first he wavered in following the Lord. Then followed months of bitter family persecution and intense peer pressure. His Bible was torn up, and he was forced to leave home. Still he stood for the Lord. He has since been able to return home, and has continued to grow and share his faith. His family has mellowed in their resistance to Christianity. Prayer played a major part in Kumar's initial response to Christ and his endurance under pressure.

The story of Kumar illustrates the following thought written by S. D. Gordon: "Prayer is striking the winning blow. . . . Service is gathering up the results."[9]

Adopt a Mission Field

The need in some countries of the world is overwhelming. Consider the most populous nations. China has approximately one billion people. India has about 700 million people, so together these two countries include over one third of the world's people. The small number of true Christians is heartbreaking. Consider greater Los Angeles with its seven million people. A comparable city in many parts of northern India would have only 350 people who were born again (one out of 20,000). Many local churches in Los Angeles have two or three times that number. Although China has a greater percentage of Christians than India does, the spiritual needs in both countries are staggering, and some nations have an even smaller proportion of believers than India or China.

Perhaps God would have you select India or China for prayer, or another needy, closed, or difficult country. You could focus prayer on one state or one city, watching for news about it. There is nothing too hard for God. He can use your prayers to crack the resistance in even the most difficult places, and you can have a part in the advance of God's kingdom among the world's unreached peoples.

A dedicated Christian girl in the eastern United States became burdened for a little-known tribe of African pygmies and responded to the Lord's promptings to pray for them. Besides praying she also wrote to missionaries in the region, sending money to help reach the tribe. But its people were nomads, constantly roaming to new areas, and the missionaries were unable to reach and evangelize them. Never strong in health, the girl prayed for years, then died. More than twenty years passed.

Then one summer a man from Gospel Recordings discovered the tribe, and using two or three interpreters, was able to record the Gospel and basic Christian truths in the tribe's language. Months later hundreds of records were made. Eventually the records and record players brought the good news of Jesus Christ to the tribe.

The response was extraordinary. As these nomadic people heard the good news in their own language, the Holy Spirit worked. Within days most of them turned to God from idols. Missionaries were amazed at the rapid and wide response—until some recalled the burden of the sickly young girl who, through prayer, had prepared the ground for this advance of the Gospel. As David Bentley-Taylor wrote,

> The power of prayer cannot be diminished by distance. It is not limited by age, infirmity, . . . political changes or restrictions. . . . The power of prayer in the life of an obedient Christian can only be undermined by neglect.

Personal Application

1. Which idea in this chapter should I incorporate into my praying for the world?
2. Is there a non-Christian country I should select for regular, concentrated prayer?

NOTES
1. John 4:35 and Matthew 13:38, NIV.
2. S. D. Gordon, *What It Will Take to Change the World* (Baker Book House, 1981), page 112.
3. S. D. Gordon, *Quiet Talks on Prayer* (Fleming H. Revell, 1903), pages 15 and 82.
4. Galatians 6:10, NIV.
5. Thomas Kelly, *A Testament of Devotion* (Harper & Row, 1941).
6. Colossians 3:17.
7. 1 Thessalonians 1:5.
8. Psalm 90:17.
9. Gordon, *Quiet Talks on Prayer*, page 19.

Appendix A

Planning Your Quiet Time

As you plan your quiet time, the following illustration can help you keep in mind the various types of prayer described on page 76.

WORSHIP GOD
Psalm 145:1-2

GIVE THANKS
1 Thessalonians 5:17

HUMBLE YOURSELF
Isaiah 57:15

Philippians 4:6-7

PRAY FOR OTHERS
2 Timothy 2:1

PRAY FOR YOURSELF
Matthew 7:1

Here are four sample quiet time plans. In writing down your personal plan, you can follow one of the samples or select ideas from several.

Plan A

- Pray briefly about my quiet time, asking God to enlighten and guide me. Remind Him that my goal is to meet with Him and get to know Him better.
- Praise God, using 1 Chronicles 29:11–12.
- Read part of a chapter or more and choose a favorite verse.
- Use thoughts from my favorite verse as a prayer starter for each item on my prayer list.
- Dedicate my day to the Lord, and pray over its details.
- Conclude with a time of thanksgiving.

Plan B

- Read Psalm 143:8–10 as a prayer.
- Pray that I will thirst more for God and know Him more fully.
- Review several verses I have memorized.
- Give thanks for specific blessings, using a list of things for which I am thankful.
- Read the Word and prayerfully meditate, writing down a thought or two.
- Use the Lord's Prayer as a base from which to branch out in prayer for myself and others.

Plan C

- Choose one song from a hymnal or chorus book and meditate on the words or sing them to the Lord.
- Ask the Lord to use His Word in my life, molding my thinking and living.
- Read a chapter in the Bible, stopping every few verses to pray for requests and people that come to mind.
- Pray through my day, asking His blessing on each activity and responsibility.
- Affirm my dependence on God and my dedication to Him.
- Thank Him for His promised sufficiency for the day.

Plan D

- Begin by praying Psalm 119:73 and 34.
- Praise God for His surpassing love and power.

- Review what stood out to me in yesterday's quiet time, praying about it again.
- Read one chapter in the Old Testament and one in the New. Record one of the following:

    a truth about God, Christ, or the Holy Spirit;

    a principle to remember;

    an example to follow;

    an error to avoid;

    a command to obey;

    a promise to depend on.
- Pray about what I wrote.
- Pray using my prayer list.

Appendix B

Remarkable Answers and Persistence

The following experiences from George Mueller's life are examples of how this man of faith repeatedly saw God work.

Providing Breakfast

Samuel Chadwick in his most inspiring book *The Path of Prayer* relates an occasion when Dr. A. T. Pierson was the guest of George Mueller at his orphanage. He says: "One night when all the household had retired he (Mueller) asked Pierson to join him in prayer. He told him that there was absolutely nothing in the house for next morning's breakfast. My friend tried to remonstrate with him and to remind him that all the stores were closed. Mueller knew all that. He had prayed as he always prayed, and he never told anyone of his needs but God. They prayed—at least Mueller did—and Pierson tried to. They went to bed and slept, and breakfast *for two thousand children was there in abundance at the usual breakfast hour.* Neither Mueller nor Pierson ever knew how the answer came. The story was told next morning to Simon Short of Bristol, under pledge of secrecy until the benefactor died. The details of it are thrilling, but all that need be told here is that the Lord called him out of bed in the middle of the night to send breakfast to Mueller's orphanage, and knowing nothing of the need, or of the two men at prayer, he sent provisions that would feed them a month. This is like the Lord God of Elijah, and still more like the God and Father of our Lord Jesus Christ."[1]

Dispelling Fog

The well-known evangelist Charles Inglis related the following incident in George Mueller's life:

When I first came to America thirty-one years ago, I crossed the Atlantic with the captain of a steamer who was one of the most devoted men I ever knew; and when we were off the banks of Newfoundland he said to me, "Mr. Inglis, the last time I crossed here, five weeks ago, one of the most extraordinary things happened that has completely revolutionized the whole of my Christian life. Up to that time I was one of your ordinary Christians. We had a man of God on board, George Mueller, of Bristol. I had been on that bridge for twenty-two hours and never left it. I was startled by someone tapping me on the shoulder. It was George Mueller.

"Captain," he said, "I have come to tell you that I must be in Quebec on Saturday afternoon." This was Wednesday.

"It is impossible," I said.

"Very well, if your ship can't take me, God will find some other means of locomotion to take me. I have never broken an engagement in fifty-seven years."

"I would willingly help you, but how can I? I am helpless."

"Let us go down to the chart room, and pray," he said.

"I looked at this man and I thought to myself, 'What lunatic asylum could the man have come from? I never heard of such a thing.'

"Mr. Mueller," I said, "do you know how dense this fog is?"

"No," he replied, "my eye is not on the density of the fog, but on the living God, who controls every circumstance of my life."

He went down on his knees, and he prayed one of the most simple prayers. I thought to myself, "That would suit a children's class, where the children were not more than eight or nine years of age." The burden of his prayer was something like this. "O Lord, if it is consistent with Thy will, please remove this fog in five minutes. You know the engagement You made for me in Quebec for Saturday. I believe it is Your will."

When he had finished, I was going to pray, but he put his hand on my shoulder and told me not to pray.

"First," he said, "you do not believe God will do it; and, second I believe He has done it. And there is no need whatever for you to pray about it."

I looked at him, and George Mueller said this, "Captain, I have known my Lord for fifty-seven years and there has never been a single day that I have failed to gain an audience with the King. Get up, Captain, and open the door, and you will find the fog is gone." I got up, and the fog *was* gone. On Saturday afternoon George Mueller was in Quebec."[2]

Winning the Lost
In commenting on the thousands of rapid answers to his prayers Mr. Mueller said,

One might suppose all my prayers have been . . . promptly answered. No, not all of them. Sometimes I have had to wait weeks, months, or years; sometimes many years.

During the first six weeks of the year 1855 I heard of the conversion of six persons for whom I had been praying for a long time. For one I had been praying between two and three years; for another I had been praying between three and four years; for another about seven years; for the fourth, ten years; for the fifth about fifteen years; and for the sixth above twenty years.

Therefore, beloved brethren and sisters, go on waiting upon God, go on praying; only be sure you ask for things which are according to the mind of God.[3]

NOTES 1. *George Mueller, Man of Faith*, edited by A. Sims (Singapore: The Navigators, n.d.), pages 20–21.
   2. Sims, pages 21–23.
   3. Roger Steer, *George Mueller: Delighted in God* (Harold Shaw Publications, 1981).

Further Reading on Prayer

Bounds, E. M.,	*Power Through Prayer* (Zondervan Publishing House, 1979). One of the great classics on prayer, full of challenges on prayer's importance and power.
Bridges, Jerry,	*How to Get Results Through Prayer* (NavPress, 1975). A brief, practical booklet on prayer.
Goforth, Rosalind,	*Goforth of China* (Bethany House Publishers, 1969). An insightful missionary biography. It shows the impact of prayer through a man saturated with the Word of God, faith, and concern for the lost.
Hallesby, O.,	*Prayer* (Augsburg Publishing House, 1975). Excellent insights and warm illustrations.
Sanders, J. Oswald,	*Prayer Power Unlimited* (Moody Press, 1979). Rich insights and helpful illustrations of many aspects of prayer.
Sanny, Lorne,	*How to Spend a Day in Prayer* (NavPress, 1979). A booklet of practical suggestions for using the day profitably.
Sims, A.,	*George Mueller, Man of Faith* (Singapore: The Navigators, n.d.). A short and challenging booklet on this man of prayer.
Steer, Roger,	*George Mueller: Delighted in God* (Harold Shaw Publications, 1981). A fresh biography describing Mr. Mueller's godliness, prayer life, faith, evangelism, and worldwide ministry.
Woods, C. Stacy, and others,	*Quiet Time* (InterVarsity Press, 1979). An outstanding booklet on the quiet time, by noted Christian leaders.

Index of Topics

Abiding in Christ
  description of, 9–10
  effects on prayer, 10–11
  first foundation of prayer, 9–13
  Hudson Taylor (illustration), 12–13
  "never be conscious of not abiding"
    (Taylor), 13
  "one with the risen . . . Savior"
    (Taylor), 13
  praying about understanding and
    hindrances, 13
  relation to God's Word, 10
  results of, 9–11, 13
  through humility and faith, 11–12
Answered prayer, examples of
  xii–xiii, 3–5, 21–22, 33–35, 49,
    106–107, 114–115, 123–125,
    136, 143, 149–151
Answered prayer, keys to
  abiding in Christ, 9–10, 25, 35–36
  arrow prayers get results,
    114–115
  Christ's empowering, 12–13
  cleansed from known sin, 15–23
  desire to know and follow Christ
    diligently, 97
  efficacy not linked to feelings, 87
  fellowship with Christ, 28–29
  foundations and conditions summa-
    rized, 25–26, 35–36
  happy dependence, 10–11
  high view of Scripture, 85–86
  pray for God's glory, 42, 125
  pray in faith, 29–35
  pray in God's will, 27–29
  pray in Jesus' name, 26–27
  pray persistently, 120–122

  right motives, 28–29
  "walk by faith" (Edman), 29
  willing to do God's will, 27–29
Arrow prayers
  114–115, 117–118, 128, 136
Bible and prayer
  contains instructions for prayer,
    25–36, 85–86
  defeats Satan, 57
  depending on the Word, not feel-
    - ings, 87–89
  describes man's lost condition, 135
  diligent, consistent intake, 82
  enriches us, 80
  "give His book first place" (James),
    83
  God's Word stimulates prayer,
    28–29
  how to meditate, 79–80
  how to read, 81–82, 147
  motivates to pray, 86
  "the listening side of prayer"
    (Gordon), 65–66
  using in prayer, 61
  "Who should read the Bible?"
    (Mears), 80–81
Body and prayer
  eyes, 113
  in any position or activity, 113
  "kneeling does matter, but" (Lewis),
    74
  variety of positions, 74
Boldness
  increased with practice in prayer,
    118
  through abiding in Christ and con-
    fessing sin, 13

Boldness (cont.)
  through Christ's death and resurrection, 7–8
Commands to pray
  actually an invitation, 86–87
  offer us partnership and refreshment, 131–132
  provide greatest motivation, 86
Concentration, helps for, 73–74
Conditions for answers
  author discovering God's will (illustration), 28
  conditions not burdensome requirements, 35
  growth in knowing God's will, 28–29
  how to use conditions, 35
  in faith, 29–30
  in God's will, 27–29
  in Jesus' name, 26–27
  not coming in our own name (Thielicke), 27
  President's son (illustration), 26–27
  signposts for effective prayer, 35
  three conditions, 25–36
  why conditions, 25–26, 35–36
Confession
  Bible teacher to ticket agent (illustration), 20
  brings God's forgiveness, 15
  confess quickly, 21–22
  Dawson Trotman's public confession (illustration), 22
  develops humility, 21
  draws God's compassion, 15
  essential for abiding in Christ, 20
  focus on personal sin, 22
  frees us to receive God's grace, 22–23
  increases others' respect for you, 20
  instant forgiveness, 22–23
  making the first move, 20–21
  probation and penance not required, 19, 22–23
  related to humbling yourself, 76
  requires humility, 19–21
  restitution, 20
  restores enjoyment of life, 22
  restores fellowship with God and man, 15–17

  simplicity of, 18, 22–23
  a step toward emotional healing (illustration), 18
  to those sinned against, 19–20
  unconfessed sin and distressing emotions, 89–90
  worth the cost, 20
Cook, Captain James, xi
David
  balanced emotions and obedience, 95
  delight in God's commands, 85
  explained his problems to God, 93
  single-minded devotion to God, 100–101
  spent time alone with God, 69
Dedication
  example of apostle Paul, 99–100
  examples of single-mindedness, 100–101
  prayer of dedication, 42
  reaffirming in quiet time, 75, 95, 146
  unreserved commitment, 41–42, 99–100
Defensive prayer
  examples of, 57–58
  pray against sin and Satan, 57–58
Dependence. See also Faith.
  acknowledge in quiet time, 75–76, 95, 146
  as dependent beings, 41
  not on our insights or abilities, 11
  not on our merits, 27
  on the Lord, 11–12
  on the Spirit, 88
  on truths of Word, 12
  on Word, not feelings, 87–89
Disappointment in prayer, 85
Doubt
  dealing with, 31
  double-minded, 31–32
  intellectual doubts, 30–31
Edwards, Jonathan
  "whether others do or not, I will," 97
Eloquence and prayer
  may enhance public praying, 92
  no influence on answers, 91–92

Emotions and prayer
 bring God into your enjoyment, 116
 compassion for the lost, 134
 depend on Word, not feelings, 87–89
 distress from unconfessed sin, 89–90
 excessive emotionalism, 93–95
 false guilt, 89–90
 fluctuating emotions are normal, 89
 "heart felt like wood" (Taylor), 89
 Holy Spirit and Word lift emotions, 91
 McComb's prayer against spiritual dry spells, 90
 pray for the lost, 134–135
 scriptural examples of emotional prayers, 87
 tears, 93–94
 true and false emotions, 93–95
 verses that encourage, 90–91
 "we should pray when" (Spurgeon), 87
Epaphras
 labored in prayer, 130
Evangelistic prayer
 examples of, xi, 4–5, 106–107, 112, 115, 119, 123, 135–137, 141–143, 151
 for world, 139–144
 makes conversion easier for the lost (Billheimer), 137
 Paul's example, 135
Faith. See also dependence.
 abiding in Christ by, 11–12
 "affectionate confidence" (Quiet time), 77
 attitude of trust, 29–30
 "authentic faith" (Halverson), 88
 choosing to trust, 12
 confidence in Christ, 11–12
 confidence in statements of God, 29–30
 connects God's power with our need, 30
 conquers giants (Edman), 29
 disobedience prevents praying in faith, 32
 examples of praying in faith, 33–35
 expectant attitude, 77

faith without feelings of certainty, 30
 general and specific faith, 33–35
 help-my-unbelief faith, 30–31
 "if I only believed" (Mueller), 34–35
 "not a force we exercise" (Hay), 29
 prayer as supremely an act of faith, 66
 prayer, the evidence of true faith, 105
 "psychological gymnastics" (Lewis), 30
 restful faith, 11–13
 rooted in God and His promises, 32–33, 34–35
 stable faith, 32–33
 sustained through God's Word, 12
 thoughts that hinder faith, 31
Favorite verse method, 67–68, 146
Fellowship and prayer. See also Quiet time.
 based on abiding and cleansing, 25
 "be much alone with God" (Bounds), 82
 broken by sin, 15
 Christ's deep desire, 97–98
 "continually conversing with Him" (Brother Lawrence), 116
 damaged by an unforgiving attitude, 52
 deepened by persistent prayer, 121–122, 125
 enriching fellowship through praise, 68–69
 examples of God's great men, 69
 "five minutes with Him" (Morgan), 110
 "he is my guest" (Munger), 97–98
 intimate fellowship with the King, 10
 muddy child restored to fellowship (illustration), 15
 need for daily fellowship, 103–110
 one method of, 65–67
 prerequisite of answered prayer, 28–29
 primary goal of quiet time, 73
 restored by confession (illustration), 16
 "we are as close to God as we

Fellowship and prayer *(cont.)*
  choose to be" (Sanders), 70
Forgiveness and prayer
  forgiven as we forgive, 51
  forgiveness and health, 16, 51
  forgiving attitude inspired by
    Christ's suffering and God's for-
    giveness, 53
  unforgiving attitude "breaks the
    bridge" (Lord Herbert), 53
  unforgiving attitude brings suffering,
    52
  unforgiving attitude hinders prayers,
    52
God, who He is
  "able and willing" (Mueller), 34–35
  affectionate and awesome, 41
  all powerful, 32–33
  allows free will, 136
  always available, 7, 10, 41, 112–113
  desires our fellowship, 73, 97–98
  desires to bless and fortify us, 69–
    70
  desires to meet with us daily, 69–
    70
  eager to hear our prayers, 8
  enriches us, 80
  "everlasting pre-occupation with
    God" (Tozer), 68
  "failure . . . to understand God . . .
    unhappiness" (Tozer), 41
  faithful to forgive confessed sin, 18
  giver of all good things, 127–128
  His will is good, 44
  ideal Father, 40–41
  involved in our trials, 55–56
  King and Supreme Ruler of all, 3–4
  longs to meet our needs, 4
  looks for wholehearted followers,
    97, 101
  loves the whole world, 139
  "loves us as though there were but
    one" (Augustine), 3
  "most winsome of all beings"
    (Tozer), 41
  the Provider, 47–50
  reasons for worshipping Him, 73
  the unsurpassed Forgiver, 53
  wants all men to be saved, 133
  worthy of praise, 59–60, 68–69

Groanings, sorrow in prayer, 93–94
Growth in prayer, 6–7, 28–29, chap-
    ters 10–20
Guidance
  as a young Christian (illustration),
    28–29
  through Spirit and Word, 28
  William Carey (illustration), xi–
    xiii
Guilt
  vague, undefined, 89–90
Hard work and prayer
  "harder now than ten years ago"
    (Sanny), 130
  in an abiding life, 11–12
  "not pleasant, dreamy reverie"
    (Sanders), 130
Hindrances to prayer
  bitterness, 16
  contentless, wordless approach,
    61–62
  covering our sins, 15
  critical spirit, no compassion, 17
  distractions, interruptions, 73–74
  double-minded doubting, 31–32
  failure to plan, 73
  neglecting God's instructions, 85
  self-sufficiency and self-pity, 13
  sin, 17
  slavery to methods, 76
  unforgiving attitude, 51–52
  unloving husbands, unsubmissive
    wives, 17
  vain repetition, 122
  wandering thoughts, 75
  "whatever weakens . . . is sin to
    you" (S. Wesley), 19
Holy Spirit and prayer
  born of, sealed, baptized, indwelt
    by, 128
  can prompt originality, 92
  Comforter, Counselor, Helper, 128
  eager to meet our needs, 128
  energizes us as we pray, 131
  evidences of being filled, 129
  fullness of, 128–130
  Holy Spirit and hard work, 131
  how to be filled, 129–130
  keeps us from sin, 29
  not author of undefined guilt, 90

prayer for the Holy Spirit, 127
renews and focuses our minds,
117
reveals sin, 89–90
sensitive to His leading, 73
"Spirit must be honored" (Murray),
127
"Spirit of the Word and prayer"
(Murray), 91
Spirit's power, our faith and labor,
132
what not to pray regarding Spirit,
128
what to pray regarding Spirit, 128
works with Word, fills with hope,
91
Honest communicating, 6, 112–113,
116
Humbling ourselves
acknowledging our inadequacy, 11
by praying for daily bread, 49–50
humble, dependent beings, 41
"humility is perfect quietness"
(Murray), 12
in our quiet time, 74, 76
related to facing sin, 19–21, 54
sustained through God's Word, 12
Husband-wife relationships, 17
Illustrations
arrow prayer brings clothes, 114
arrow prayer, conversion of college
friend, 115
arrow prayer prevents accident, 114
atheistic congressman, 4–5
author discovers God's will, 28
Bible teacher's confession to ticket
agent, 20
comparing prayer to ordering a
hamburger, 61
confession helps bring emotional
healing, 18
Dawson Trotman's public confession, 22
diamond mine, 80
evangelistic movie on campus,
106–107
George Mueller's prayer about fog,
124, 150–151
George Mueller's prayer about food,
123–124, 149–150

Hudson Taylor's secret of abiding in
Christ, 12–13
Indian couple using neighborhood
map, 141–142
Indonesian and suitcase, 3–4
John Ridgway and crown prince of
Thailand, 10
man saved after ten years of prayer,
136
meeting financial needs, 48, 124
muddy child restored to fellowship,
15
prayers of jogging neighbor, 123
praying in faith nonspecifically,
33–34
President's son, 26–27
private line to heaven, 112
provision of a car, 34
provision of a home to rent, 49
pygmy tribe converted, 143
reading Bible as more than history
book, 68
repeating Lord's prayer 3000 times,
122
Ruth Graham and open Bibles,
109
Satan like a tiger, 133–134
statue and false worship, 94
Susannah Wesley's apron, 109
twenty-seven years of bitterness, 16
William Carey's praying sister,
xii–xiii
woman moderating emotions,
94–95
woman needing operation, 16
wronged person appears after
prayer, 21–22
young Hindu prodigy, 94
Intensity in prayer, 92–93
Jesus Christ and prayer
empowering through, 13
enchantment alone insufficient, 95
His foot washing (spiritual cleansing), 18–19
His teaching on prayer, 37, 119–
121, 127–128
Hudson Taylor's secret of abiding in,
12–13
made access possible, 7–8, 10,
18–19

Jesus Christ and prayer *(cont.)*
  made time to pray, 69, 105
  need to abide in, 9–13
  never yielded to sin, 56
  our adequacy in, 11
  "a passion for Christ" (Quiet Time),
    101–102
  praying in Jesus' name, 26–27
  recalling His suffering, cure for re-
    sentment, 53
  sufficient for all our needs, 149–150
  yearns for our fellowship, 97–98
Long prayers
  benefits of, 93
  brevity of Lord's prayer, 60
  not a condition for answers, 93
Maharaj, Rabindranath R., 94
Meditation
  commanded in Scripture, 79
  how, 79, 82–83
Methods
  coupled with Spirit's leading, 73
  not become slave to, 76
  planning of quiet time, 146–147
  their place in quiet time, 73
Moravians, 101
Motivation for prayer
  brings joy to God, 41
  brings subjective benefits, 6
  brings us to the living God, 7
  colaboring with God's great plan,
    xiii, 131–132
  effectiveness not dependent on feel-
    ings, 87
  God longs for a relationship with us,
    121
  God longs to give good things, 121
  God longs to hear us, 6
  God surpasses our ideal Father, 41
  heavenly rewards, xiii
  influences world, xiii–xiv
  mature praying comes with practice,
    6–7
  prayer a burden only as wings to an
    airplane, 132
  simple and enjoyable, 5–7
  stimulated by God's commands,
    86–87
  through becoming informed,
    139–140

Mystery of prayer
  can pray without full understand-
    ing, 6–7, 129–130
  paradox: God's grace and hard
    work, 131
Nehemiah
  illustration of arrow prayers,
    111–112
  illustration of prayer and hard work,
    131
Obedience and prayer
  active acceptance of God's plans, 44
  by abiding in Christ and cleansing
    from sin, 9, 23
  disobedience prevents praying in
    faith, 32
Patience in prayer
  developed through persistence,
    121–122
  necessary to grow in prayer, 6
Paul the apostle
  his compassion and prayer for the
    lost, 135
  his conversion, 99–100
  his one purpose, 100
Persistence in prayer
  changes us, not God, 121–122
  deepens fellowship, 121–122
  develops faith, perseverance, charac-
    ter, 122
  examples, 122–125
  for the lost, 135–136
  George Mueller's examples, 119,
    124, 151
  helps overcome impatience, in-
    creases trust, 122
  not mindless repetition, 122
  taught by Christ, 119, 121
Peter the apostle
  his arrow prayer, 114
  his wavering faith, 30–31
Place for praying
  advantage of regular place, 73–74
  anywhere, 111–118
  as private as possible, 74
Positions. See Body and Prayer.
Praise
  examples of, 41–42, 59
  honors God, 74–75
  how to enrich your praise, 68–69

in quiet time, 146–147
on need to praise throughout day, 116
owed to God, 54
prevents preoccupation with self, 74

Prayer lists
how to use effectively, 75–76

Praying cobbler, xi–xiii

Praying for myself
about my quiet time, 77
briefly, while working or walking, 6
defensive prayer, 57–58
desires molded, 10
for a specific blessing (Mueller), 124
for bills to be paid (illustration), 48
for clean conscience and life, 54
for daily needs, 47–48
for deliverance from Satan, 56–57
for deliverance in temptation, 55–56
for financial needs (illustration), 124
for God's glory, not "to wrest advantages" (Hallesby), 42
for guidance regarding service, 141
for housing (illustration), 49
for practical things (illustration), 34
for refreshment in dry times, 90
for "sensitivity to sin" (C. Wesley), 55
for spiritual and emotional needs, 49
regarding my praying for the lost, 136
sharing thoughts, feelings, problems, 5
that God will reveal sin, 19, 32, 89–90
that I will advance His kingdom, 43
that I will honor Him, 42
that I will learn to abide, 13
that I will learn to pray, 7
through the Lord's prayer, 62
to know God's will (illustration), 28
when I have plenty, 48
with arrow prayers, 114–115
"Your will be done in me," 44

Praying for others. See also Evangelistic prayer.
brief prayer, examples, 61
for physical needs, 140–141
for son and daughter (illustration), 124–125
for workers in His kingdom, 143
helpfulness of prayer lists, pictures, 75
selectively, 135–136, 141
"someone miles and years away" (Goforth), 111
through arrow prayers, 111–112
what to pray, 44, 76
who to include, 44, 75–76
with persistence, 119–120

Quiet time
aids to alertness, concentration, 73–75
begin with prayer, 66
cultivate good habits, 77
examples from Scripture, 69
expectant attitude, 77
favorite verses, 66–67
how to have, 65–70
how to help others in, 67–68
how to plan, 146–147
importance of, 69–70
importance of planning for, 73
importance of Spirit's leading in, 73
include praise, 68–69
include several types of prayer, 76
keep a notebook, 67
making time for, 103–110
marking Bible, 66
"must simplify our lives" (Tozer), 70
not "just business" (Quiet Time), 68
positions of body, 74
pray about it, 77
prepare your heart for, 74–75
primary goal in, 73
"Speak, Lord, in the stillness" (song), 66
use favorite verses in prayer, 67–68
use pictures, 75
use prayer lists, 75–76
variety, 76–77
where to have, 73–74

Rewards for prayer
sharing the rewards of missionaries, xiii

Satan
defeated by Word and prayer, 57

Satan *(cont.)*
  finds our weak points, 57–58
  his temptations accompany every
    testing, 55–56
  his use of sin to hinder prayer,
    15–16
  like Vietnamese tiger (illustration),
    133–134
  confuses God's way with his, 70
  tempts to trust in feelings, not Word,
    88–89
  the vicious attacker, 56–57
Simplicity of prayer
  brevity of Lord's prayer, 60
  illustrations, 5–6, 60–61
  Nehemiah's short, concise prayers,
    111–112
  "we make it too complicated"
    (Redpath), 61
Sin and prayer
  breaks our intimacy with God, 17
  damage to effectiveness, family, 16
  damage to health, 16
  importance of cleansing, 15–17
  "refusing to wait" (Halverson), 122
  results of not forgiving, 52
  results of willful independence, 40
  "a sensitivity to sin" (C. Wesley), 55
  sins of omission, 53–54
  "whatever weakens . . . is sin to
    you" (S. Wesley), 19
Specific prayer
  be selective in specific prayer for
    world, 141
  examples, xi–xiii, 3–5, 48–49,
    114–115, 149–151
  for specific lost people, 135–136
Struggles, imperfections, failures, 27,
  53–54
Subjective benefits of prayer, xiii, 6, 8,
  49–50, 69–70, 85, 90–91, 93, 104–
  105, 116–117, 121–122, 131–132
Temptation
  God's purposes in, 55
  importance of refusing compromise,
    56
  not toying with temptation, 56
  preparing for it through prayer, 56
  Satan's purposes in, 55
Thanksgiving

  honoring God, 74–75
  including in quiet time, 76, 146
  need and command to give thanks
    throughout day, 116
  owed to God, 54
Time and prayer
  "chinks of time" (Laubach), 115
  consistent time, 106
  "continually conversing with Him"
    (Brother Lawrence), 116
  extended times, 107–108
  "five minutes with Him" (Morgan),
    110
  "the great people of the earth"
    (Gordon), xiv
  "how little time" (Torrey), 103
  length, 106, 111
  "little estimate" (Bounds), 103
  making time, 103–110
  "men who have done the most"
    (Bounds), 108
  redeeming the time, 115
  "things that are most important"
    (Bach), 65
  which time of day, 108–109,
    113–114
Types of prayer, 76
Unbelief
  cultivated by doubting and fearful
    thoughts, 31
  handling doubting thoughts, 31
  "help my unbelief," 30
  Peter's unbelief, 31
  rooted in disobedience, 32
Unceasing prayer
  after every sin, 116
  "chinks of time" (Laubach), 115
  keeps confidence centered in God,
    116
  redirect your thoughts, 117
  select a basic arrow prayer, 117–118
  thanksgiving throughout day, 116
  through arrow prayers, 117–118
  through Scripture memory, 117
Variety
  can be prompted by Holy Spirit, 92
  no influence on answers, 92
  prayer more than making requests, 5
  types of prayer, 76
  value in quiet time, 76–77

Wesley, John
  his single-minded devotion to
    Christ, 101
Who we are in Christ
  adequate, 11
  branches in Vine, 9
  children of God, 7–8, 27
  insiders in court of heaven, 7–8
  no longer strangers, now members
    and citizens, 8
  one with Christ, 12–13
  privileged ones, 134–135
  righteous, 18
  royalty, 10
  totally forgiven, 7, 51
Will of God and prayer
  "begins with God's interests"
    (Morgan), 47
  discovered by alignment with God's
    purposes, 44
  learning God's will, 27–29
  need to pray in His will, 25
  persistent prayer does not change
    God's will, but us, 121–122
  praying according to Scripture,
    27–28
  praying from a clean heart, 13–14
Word of God. See Bible and prayer.
Wordless prayer
  dangers of, 61–62
  quietness, 6
World vision

"continents, not peanuts"
    (Trotman), 139
"direct, dynamic touch with a
    world" (Gordon), 140
importance of selective involve-
    ment, 141
information essential, 139–140
"mightiest factor in world revolu-
    tion" (Redpath), 44
our part in Great Commission, 139
partnership in God's planet-sized
    purposes (Gordon), 140
prayer connecting us with God's
    world purpose, xiii
praying for secular world, 44
"reaching mission field on our
    knees" (Fraser), xiii
"striking the winning blow"
    (Gordon), 142
Thy kingdom come, 43
William Carey's example, xi
world not abandoned to the devil
    (Redpath), 43
Worship
  importance of, 68
  one basic type of prayer, 76
  pleases God, 73
  prepares heart for quiet time, 74–75
  sample prayers of worship, 41–42
  "Thine is the kingdom," 59–60
Zinzendorf, Count
  his single-minded devotion to
    Christ, 101

Index of Quotations
and References to People

Augustine
  "loves us as though there were but one," 3
Author unknown
  "Speak, Lord, in the stillness," 66
  "Thou art coming to a king" (old hymn), 3
Bach, T. J.
  "things that are most important," 65
Bentley-Taylor, David
  power of prayer limited only by neglect, 143
Bernard of Clairvaux
  "We taste Thee . . . and long to feast upon Thee still," 49
Billheimer, Paul E.
  on making conversion easier for the lost, 137
Bounds, E. M.
  "the little estimate we put on prayer," 103
  "men who have done the most," 108
  "much alone with God," 82
Brooks, Phillips
  "God's mercy seat is no mere stall," 25
Brother Lawrence
  "continually conversing with Him," 116
Carey, William
  "Expect great things from God," xii
  "I am not gifted," xii
Chambers, Oswald

on being changed by Jesus versus mere enchantment, 95
Cook, James, xi
Count Zinzendorf
  his single-minded devotion to Christ, 101
Eastman, Dick
  on Hudson Taylor's "emotionless prayer," 89
Edman, V. Raymond
  "walk by faith," 29
Edwards, Jonathan
  "Whether others do or not, I will," 97
Einstein, Albert
  "perfection of means and confusion of goals," 103
Ellul, Jacques
  on prayer as a liberating opportunity, 86
  "the vast silence . . . the incommunicable," 61–62
Fraser, J. O.
  "reaching mission fields on our knees," xiii
Gilmour, James
  "waiting for Elijah to call," 110
Goforth, Mrs. Jonathan
  "a thought of someone miles and years away," 111
Gordon, S. D.
  "direct, dynamic touch with a world," 140
  "The faith that believes . . . not born in a hurry," 33

Gordon, S. D. *(cont.)*
"the great people of the earth," xiv
"the listening side of prayer," 65–66
"simple surrender . . . to the higher will," 5
"striking the winning blow," 142
"Thou knowest both ends of prayer," 7
Graham, Ruth
open Bibles around the house, 109
Gurnall, William
"as if the gilding of the key," 92
Guyon, Madam
"too much taken up with my interior joys," 94
Hallesby, O.
"Make use of prayer, not to wrest . . . advantages," 42
Halverson, Richard C.
"authentic faith," 87
"One may sin . . . by refusing to wait," 122
Hansen, Howard
on God's forgiveness inspiring us to forgive, 52–53
prayer not "limited to the wild blue yonder," 47
Hay, Alexander R.
"Faith is not a force we exercise," 29
Head of a hospital
"I could dismiss . . . patients tomorrow," 51
James, J. S.
"Give His book first place," 83
Kelly, Thomas
God "portions out His vast concern into bundles," 141
Laubach, Frank
"Acquire a new way of thinking," 117
"chinks of time," 115
Lewis, C. S.
on faith not being "psychological gymnastics," 30
"Kneeling does matter, but," 74
Lord Herbert
Unforgiving attitude "breaks the bridge," 53
Maharaj, Rabindranath R., 94

McComb, Samuel
a prayer against spiritual dry spells, 90
Mears, Henrietta
"Who should read the Bible?" 80–81
Morgan, G. Campbell
"five minutes with Him," 110
on God's interests first, then man's needs, 47
Mueller, George
"God is able and willing," 34–35
"Never give up until the answer comes," 119
prayer about fog, 124, 150–151
prayer about food, 123–124, 149–150
waited three years and ten months before blessing given, 124
Munger, Robert
"He is my guest," 97–98
Murray, Andrew
"Humility is perfect quietness," 12
on the Spirit as Leader and Director of entire walk, 127
"Spirit of the Word and prayer," 91
Newton, Isaac
"on the edge of an ocean of truth," 59
Quiet Time
"affectionate confidence," 77
"a passion for Christ," 101–102
"We are burdened with requests," 68
Redpath, Alan
"mightiest factor in world revolution," 44
"We make it too complicated," 61
world not abandoned to the devil, 43
Ridgway, John
crown prince of Thailand, 10
Sanders, J. Oswald
on God tests, but the devil tempts, 55
on Lord's prayer as "a pattern, not an inflexible form," 39
prayer "not pleasant, dreamy reverie," 130

"We are as close to God as we *choose* to be," 70

Sanny, Lorne
prayer "harder now than ten years ago," 130

Spurgeon, Charles H.
"We should pray when," 87

Taylor, Hudson
on abiding in Christ, 12–13
"Heart felt like wood when praying," 89
"Never be conscious of not abiding," 13
"one with the risen . . . Savior," 13

Thielicke, Helmut
on not coming in our own name, 27

Torrey, R. A.
"too busy to pray . . . too busy to have power," 103

Tozer, A. W.
"everlasting preoccupation with God," 68

"failure . . . to understand God . . . unhappiness," 41
"The heart . . . is like a musical instrument," 94
"most winsome of all beings," 41
"must simplify our lives," 70

Trotman, Dawson
"continents, not peanuts," 139
"Our most difficult work . . . is prayer," 132
public confession, 22

Wesley, Charles
"a sensitivity to sin," 55

Wesley, John
his single-minded devotion to Christ, 101

Wesley, Suzannah
her apron, 109
"Whatever weakens . . . is sin to you," 19

Index of Scripture References

Exodus 15:11 **68**
  20:4–5 **94**
Deuteronomy 1:32–33 **49**
Joshua 1:8 **79**
1 Samuel 30:24 **xiii**
1 Chronicles 29:11–12 **146**
  29:11–13 **59**
2 Chronicles 16:9 **97**
Nehemiah 2:4 **112**
  4:9 **131**
  6:9 **112**
  13:31 **112**
Psalm 1:1–3 **79**
  12:6 **85**
  16:6 **90**
  19:12 **90**
  19:14 **53**
  23:6 **91**
  27:4, 8 **101**
  31:19 **90**
  32:5 **15, 18**
  37:4 **10**
  43:4 **6**
  62:8 **6**
  65:5 **42**
  66:18 **17**
  86:5 **54**
  90:14 **73**
  90:17 **141**
  99:2–3 **42**
  103:1–2 **42**
  103:1–5 **69**
  111:3, 9 **42**
  119:24 **86**
  119:34 **80, 146**
  119:45 **86**
  119:47–48 **86**

  119:59–60 **95**
  119:73 **146**
  119:128 **85**
  119:151 **85**
  119:160 **85**
  127:1 **104**
  130:3–4 **53**
  139:23–24 **32**
  143:8–10 **65, 146**
  145:3 **68**
  145:17–19 **69**
Proverbs 4:23 **82**
  11:24–25 **48**
  13:19 **81**
  19:17 **48**
  28:13 **15, 16**
Song of Solomon 2:14 **97**
Isaiah 9:6–7 **43**
  35:8 **54**
  42:8 **58**
  43:25 **7**
  50:4 **69**
  53:5 **7**
  58 **17**
  58:2 **93**
  58:3 **93**
  58:9 **17**
  59:1–2 **17**
  62:6–7 **122**
  65:24 **114**
Jeremiah 33:3 **86**
Daniel 6:10 **69**
  7:9–10 **60**
Zechariah 4:6 **91, 93**
Malachi 1:11 **42**
Matthew 5:23–24 **20**
  6:6 **74**

Matthew (cont.)
  6:7 **122**
  6:9–13 **39**
  6:11 **47**
  6:12 **51**
  6:31–33 **48**
  6:33 **48**
  7:9 **127**
  7:24–25 **85**
  9:36 **133**
  13:38 **139**
  13:58 **30**
  14:22–33 **30**
  14:28–31 **114**
  17:20 **21**
  18:15 **21**
  18:35 **52**
  21:22 **29**
  26:41 **56, 86**
Mark 1:35 **69**
  9:24 **30**
Luke 1:37 **60**
  1:45 **21**
  5:15–16 **105**
  6:12 **105**
  11:4 **51**
  11:5–8 **119**
  11:9 **86**
  11:9–10 **120**
  11:10 **13**
  11:11–13 **127**
  18:1 **86, 125**
John 1:12 **128**
  3:3–7 **128**
  3:36 **135**
  4:14 **129**
  4:35 **139**
  6:35 **49**
  7:38 **129**
  13:8 **18**
  13:10 **19**
  14:13–14 **26**
  15:5 **11, 131**
  15:7 **9, 28**
  16:8–9 **128**
  16:24 **6, 86**
Acts 1:8 **128**
  3:19 **77**
  10:43 **128**
  13:22 **100**

  22:6–8 **99**
  22:10 **99**
Romans 4:8 **51**
  4:20–21 **32**
  8:9 **128**
  8:15 **40**
  8:16–17 **10**
  8:33 **57**
  10:1 **135**
  11:22 **90**
  11:33 **80**
  14:5 **109**
  15:4 **91**
  15:13 **91, 128**
1 Corinthians 3:16 **128**
  10:13 **56**
  12:13 **128**
  15:10 **91**
  15:33 **56**
2 Corinthians 3:17–18 **129**
  5:18–20 **134**
  5:21 **18**
  9:6–11 **48**
  10:5 **137**
Galatians 5:14 **52**
  5:22–23 **129**
  6:1–2 **21**
  6:10 **141**
Ephesians 1:13 **128**
  1:15–16 **122**
  2:2–3 **70**
  2:12 **134**
  2:13 **7**
  2:19 **8**
  3:20 **35**
  4:26 **22**
  4:32 **53**
  5:18 **129**
  5:18–6:10 **129**
  5:22–33 **17**
  6:18 **88**
Philippians 1:9 **67**
  1:12 **4**
  1:20 **66**
  2:14–15 **67**
  3:7–10, 13–14 **100**
  3:10 **67**
  4:6 **4**
  4:13 **11, 118**
Colossians 1:9 **122**

2:6 **11**
3:2 **117**
3:17 **141**
4:2 **131**
4:12 **122**
4:12–13 **130**
1 Thessalonians 1:5 **141**
  5:17 **86, 113**
  5:18 **116**
2 Thessalonians 1:8–9 **135**
1 Timothy 2:1, 3–6 **133**
2 Timothy 2:1 **23**
  3:16–17 **82**
Hebrews 4:16 **7, 112**

10:14 **7**
10:19, 21–22 **23**
11:6 **105**
12:2 **12**
James 1:6–8 **32**
  4:6 **21, 50**
  5:16 **93**
1 Peter 2:9 **82**
  3:7 **17**
  5:5 **21**
  5:8–9 **57**
1 John 1:9 **18, 20**
  3:21–22 **14**
  5:14 **27**